MW00773920

MAKING SENSE OF REALITY

For Doug with love that is real in its consequences

MAKING SENSE OF REALITY

CULTURE AND PERCEPTION
IN EVERYDAY LIFE

TIA DENORA

Los Angeles | London | New Delhi
Singapore | Washington DC

MTSU Library
Middle Tennessee State University
Murfreesboro, Tennessee

Los Angeles | London | New Delhi
Singapore | Washington DC

SAGE Publications Ltd
1 Oliver's Yard
55 City Road
London EC1Y 1SP

SAGE Publications Inc.
2455 Teller Road
Thousand Oaks, California 91320

SAGE Publications India Pvt Ltd
B 1/I 1 Mohan Cooperative Industrial Area
Mathura Road
New Delhi 110 044

SAGE Publications Asia-Pacific Pte Ltd
3 Church Street
#10-04 Samsung Hub
Singapore 049483

Editor: Chris Rojek
Editorial assistant: Gemma Shields
Production editor: Katherine Haw
Copyeditor: Jane Fricker
Marketing manager: Michael Ainsley
Cover design: Lisa Wells-Harper
Typeset by: C&M Digitals (P) Ltd, Chennai, India
Printed in India at Replika Press Pvt Ltd

© Tia DeNora 2014

First published 2014

Apart from any fair dealing for the purposes of resea
or private study, or criticism or review, as permitted ι
the Copyright, Designs and Patents Act, 1988, this
publication may be reproduced, stored or transmittec
any form, or by any means, only with the prior perm
in writing of the publishers, or in the case of reprogr
reproduction, in accordance with the terms of licenc
issued by the Copyright Licensing Agency. Enquiries
concerning reproduction outside those terms should
sent to the publishers.

Library of Congress Control Number: 201493255

British Library Cataloguing in Publication data

A catalogue record for this book is available from
the British Library

ISBN 978-1-4462-0199-2
ISBN 978-1-4462-0200-5 (pbk)

At SAGE we take sustainability seriously. Most of our products are printed in the UK using FSC papers and board
When we print overseas we ensure sustainable papers are used as measured by the Egmont grading system.
We undertake an annual audit to monitor our sustainability.

If a scientist states it as an axiom that the sensations of heat and light which we feel correspond to some objective cause, he does not conclude that this is what it appears to the senses to be … [S]ociety cannot make its influence felt unless it is in action, and it is not in action unless the individuals who compose it are assembled together and act in common. It is by common action that it takes consciousness of itself and realizes its position; it is before all else an active cooperation. The collective ideas and sentiments are even possible only owing to these exterior movements which symbolise them, as we have established. Then it is action that dominates the religious life, because of the mere fact that it is society which is its source.

Emile Durkheim, *The Elementary Forms of Religious Life*, pp. 417–18

CONTENTS

LIST OF FIGURES

ABOUT THE AUTHOR

Tia DeNora is Professor of Sociology in SPA (Sociology, Philosophy and Anthropology) at Exeter University where she directs the SocArts Research Group. Her main area of research is music sociology where, most recently, she has completed a longitudinal study of music and well-being in collaboration with Gary Ansdell, a music therapist at Nordoff Robbins. Her books include *Beethoven and the Construction of Genius* (University of California Press, 1995), *Music in Everyday Life* (Cambridge University Press, 2000), *Music-in-Action* (Ashgate, 2011), *Music Asylums: Wellbeing Through Music in Everyday Life* (Ashgate, 2013) and *After Adorno: Rethinking Music Sociology* (Cambridge University Press, 2003), which received honourable mention for the American Sociological Association's Mary Douglas Prize for Best Book. With Gary Ansdell, she co-edits the Ashgate Series on *Music and Change: Ecological Perspectives*.

PREFACE AND ACKNOWLEDGEMENTS, OR MUSIC, MUCUS AND 'CALIFORNIA SOCIOLOGY'

This book represents a sort of intellectual 'homecoming' for me. Between 1983 and 1989 while a PhD student at the University of California, San Diego (UCSD), I had the great fortune to study ethnomethodology with Hugh ('Bud') Mehan, cognitive sociology with Aaron Cicourel, and science and technology studies (STS) with Bruno Latour. It was at UCSD that I learned that perspectives from STS, cognitive sociology and ethnomethodology, as they focused on the local and routine production of 'reality', could be really useful for the development of music sociology. Those perspectives pointed to a focus on, among other things, how people encounter, use, tinker with and adjust to objects as they make their social worlds, and with those worlds, each other.

Working on the research for what eventually became my first book (*Beethoven and the Construction of Genius* [1995]), I used this focus to consider how an environment conducive to the perception of Beethoven's talent emerged and came to be developed. That environment drew music critical discourse, musical performance practices and embodied techniques of keyboard display into mutual reference with social networks, economic arrangements of musical patronage, and the material world of music-making, most notably changes in piano technology as Beethoven lobbied early on in his career for a more 'Beethoven-friendly' instrument. The growth of this environment was integral to Beethoven's creative endeavours and to the perception of these endeavours. It also served as a foil against which the talents of his pianistic competitors could be, and were, downplayed. The key point here was that material and aesthetic environments are selectively nurturing; they allow some individuals, activities and forms of design a certain *space* – within which to be and grow (and grow in some directions). And they allocate this space differentially, to some people, projects and things at the expense of others. This often-tacit distribution of opportunities for growth, and its withholding, is, in other words, a key topic for sociology.

While completing the book on Beethoven's music, and thanks to advice from two new colleagues at Cardiff, Paul Atkinson (who had himself recently written about ethnomethodology for the *Annual Review of Sociology* [Atkinson, 1988]) and Sara Delamont (then writing on gender and education [Delamont, 1989]), I began to work on a topic more firmly lodged within gender studies and STS.

That study focused on knowledge-based controversies associated with so-called 'natural family planning' and its basis in the minute monitoring of cervical mucus secretions during the menstrual cycle. I was interested in how knowledge, indeed predictive knowledge, about the fertile female body could be produced sensorially and through seemingly 'low tech' bodily technologies.[1]

Working on both of these projects at the same time (Beethoven's reputation, and fertility awareness contraception and its reputation), my touch-typing often transposed the words music and mucus, leading to seemingly absurd turns of phrase, for example, 'Beethoven's *Mucus*' and 'Cervical *Music*'. In a funny way, this mix-up only highlighted what, for me at least, these seemingly unrelated studies held in common, namely, the focus on identities and reputations as they come to be formed and take on established, often institutionalised, realities within ecological milieux. So, as certain practices and human/non-human networks came to be regularly patterned, it became increasingly difficult *not* to see Beethoven as a genius, increasingly difficult *not* to determine that cervical mucus contraception was ineffective. These realities had become, in effect, self-evident. How then to begin to unpick the history of their facticity?

It is here that ethnomethodology (and its associated perspectives such as cognitive sociology and STS) can help. The term 'ethnomethodology' means, literally, the study of the folk ('ethno') methods by which realities are contested, created, recreated, performed and enacted over time and space – the means by which our semblance of a natural, normal world of affairs is routinely and regularly produced and reproduced. This is the perspective that will inform much of what I shall describe in what follows. But it is a perspective often grossly misunderstood within the human sciences. It is therefore worth pausing for a moment to consider some of those misunderstandings as they make their appearance in the annals of learned journals and reviews.

First, ethnomethodology is often misinterpreted as saying nothing more than that people make up reality out of nowhere as they go along. Associated with this misconception, ethnomethodology has been often (and somewhat flippantly) dismissed as 'California sociology', that is, a mode of understanding practised in the precarious and occasionally fey cultural territory of the westernmost American state (Lemert, 2002: ix; Linstead, 2006: 400). As such, ethnomethodology is identified with individualist, idealist and mentalist conceptions of reality (Maynard and Clayman, 1991: 386), as if reality were dependent upon nothing more than assertions and accounts, a kind of weak version of labelling theory, an 'I say/you say' programme of research. As I shall explain, I do not share this vision.

While there was indeed a time when most ethnomethodologists were based in California, that is no longer the case. Moreover, the accusations of individualism, of a mentalist understanding of social action, and a talk-centred focus, cannot be fully squared with ethnomethodology's obvious concern with craft practice, skill and human–object relations (resonating in turn with studies that examine our everyday encounters with the material world [see de Certeau on this point, 2011(1984): xi]). Yet more to the point, these misconceptions of ethnomethodology are contradicted in even the earliest statements of what ethnomethodology was about. For example:

> The objective reality of social facts as an ongoing accomplishment of the concerted activities of daily life, with the ordinary, artful ways of that accomplishment being by members known, used and taken for granted is, for members doing sociology, a fundamental phenomenon. (Garfinkel, 1967: vii)

In short, most ethnomethodologically inclined scholars have tended to define ethnomethodology as the *re-specification* of our methods for knowing and measuring the world (Cicourel, 1964), for acquiring a sense of social structure (Cicourel, 1974) and for 'work[ing] out' Durkheim's aphorism that we treat social facts as things (Garfinkel, 2002: 1). This working-out involves a mode of study devoted to the collaborative and craft practices by which the world as it 'is' comes to be produced. Thus, this re-specification is very different from the idea that reality is whatever I or you deem it to be because it is concerned with the (reality of) specific and trans-individual practices (craft practices – e.g., ways of handling materials and objects, ways of perceiving) by which realities take on their self-evident and often thing-like realness.[2] It is also not synonymous with phenomenological studies of perceptions and experiences of reality reported by individual research respondents. By contrast, as just stated, it consists of a focus on how experiences are actually effected and enacted, how they are produced; and that question points to new answers to ontological questions along the lines of, what kind of reality is reality?

To explore this 'working-out' or, as I will call it, the study of how we 'make sense of reality', I shall mobilise a number of case study examples, drawn from the rich and varied seam of sociology. Although I will begin and end with examples from my home field of socio-music studies (because I believe that music is good for sociology to think with), a good many of my examples will be drawn from work expressly devoted to the study of sex and gender, age, aesthetics and material culture, and disability studies. I will also draw upon case studies from the sociology of health and illness, embodiment, organisational culture and neuropsychology. The aim of this slightly magpie tactic is to provide tasting-sized portions of what sociology can show, and what it can do. It is, I think, a scholarly version of curating (Acord, 2010) and as such I hope will result in something that amounts to more than the sum of its parts. I will have more to say (and try to say it more simply) when I lay out the argument of this book in the introductory chapter.

But first there are people to thank. I am grateful to Chris Rojek for suggesting that I might write a book about, as we initially conceived it, social framing. And to Chris' brilliant colleague at Sage, editor Gemma Shields, who offered really helpful editorial suggestions, technical guidance and wisdom at every stage. Thanks as well to the other members of the Sage team: Katherine Haw, Jane Fricker, Michael Ainsley, Jonathan Hopkins for proofreading and Elizabeth Ball for the index. I am also grateful to Sage's seven anonymous reviewers who read the initial proposal (yes, even the one who suggested that Sage reject it so as to 'save trees'!) and to the three who read the full book: your help was great! At Exeter I want to thank Nigel Pleasants, Giovanna Colombetti, David Inglis, Tom Rice, Brian Rappert, and Dana Wilson-Kovacs, as well as former colleagues Robert Witkin and Barry Barnes. I also want to thank the current and past members of SocArts: Sophia Acord, Rita Gracio Alberto, Kari Batt-Rawden, Arild Bergh, Pedro dos Santos Boia, Elizabeth Dennis, Sigrun Lilja Einarsdottir, Pinar Guran, Trever Hagen, Mariko Hara, Rosanna Mead, Simon Procter, Craig Robertson, Evan Schurig, Sarah Smith, Ian Sutherland and Susan Trythall. I am also grateful to the sixty-something philosophy and sociology students who signed up for 'Knowing the Social World' in the autumn of 2011, 2012 and 2013 (it is true that you never really understand something until you've tried to explain it to someone else) and especially to James Berry, Exeter Class of 2013 (Flexible Combined Honours Programme in Psychology and Philosophy). James read the penultimate draft from the perspective of a 'student user', and his very helpful comments on how a student might navigate this text are incorporated in this final version. Thanks also to Paul Atkinson, Sara Delamont, Giampietro Gobo, Harvey Greisman (who on hearing the title suggested that the best way to write the book would be as a DIY manual) and Barry Saferstein and especially to my research partner, music therapist Gary Ansdell at the Nordoff Robbins London Centre who very generously read and commented on an early draft. Discussions in the ESRC Seminar on Arts, Health and Wellbeing, and the AHRC Network, Being in the Zone, were inspiring – thank you to all the participants. As always, at home, my gratitude goes to my husband Douglas Tudhope. If this book 'makes (any) sense' in making sense of reality, it will be due to the efforts of all of the above. I remain grateful for their help.

Exeter, January 2014

Notes

1. The project was funded by the ESRC. Cyclically produced cervical mucus can be sampled manually, held between the fingers and examined for its texture (stretchy, slippery, tacky?), smell (acid or vanilla?) and sight (clear, cloudy, white, cream?). It is not 'high tech'; it does not require urinary dipsticks, aspirations or blood samples. However, the terms 'high tech' or 'low tech' presume too much in advance, since bodily technologies are also highly sophisticated, and may be easier (and less expensive) to sustain and maintain. Their 'effectiveness' however is more highly dependent upon the lay expertise of their users (DeNora, 1996).

2. See also, for example, Zimmerman and Wieder's (1971: 285) reply to the suggestion that ethnomethodologists seek 'a solution to the problem of order in terms of "rules, norms, definitions and meanings"'. They argued that this conception of ethnomethodology 'severely delimits our central phenomenon, at the same time turning it into an essentially unquestioned resource for analysis'.

ACKNOWLEDGEMENTS

The quote from Emile Durkheim's *Elementary Forms* is reproduced with permission from Oxford University Press.
Figure 1.1 is reproduced with permission from Daniel Simons.
Figures 8.1 and 8.2 were first published in Wittgenstein, Ludwig (2009) *Philosophische Untersuchungen/Philosophical Investigations*. Revised fourth edition. Oxford: Wiley-Blackwell. Reprinted with kind permission from Wiley.

INTRODUCTION: REALITY IN EVERYDAY LIFE

This is a fairly short book addressed to what might seem like an unwieldy question – the nature of reality in everyday life. As I will suggest, the answer to this question can be made more manageable (and kept fairly compact too) if, instead of asking *what* reality is, we ask *how* our sense of reality is generated.

That question considers the ways that realities are brought into being *as* realities and how, at least some of the time, that reality may be palpable. As I shall argue, this 'how' question is emphatically one that needs sociology, albeit a sociology informed by other disciplines, perhaps especially science and technology studies, philosophy, anthropology, social psychology, neuroscience and history, the last including histories of the immediate past as it is converted into present, and future, events.

As I shall describe, this question is 'for' sociology in two senses. First, it highlights what sociology (as opposed to, say, history, economics or political science) can do. Second, and perhaps more importantly, it is 'for' sociology because it is a topic 'made for' that discipline, as it considers real-time practices, noting specifically the reality-making work that people do, and the objects, tools and sensory and aesthetic media that are drawn upon for this work as it is practised on a daily basis.

The focus on that daily basis, the so-called quotidian or the everyday, is vital here. And yet, with some notable exceptions (Goffman, 1959; Lefebvre, 1971 [1968]; Douglas, 1971 [1971], 2010 [1971]; de Certeau, 2011 [1984]; Shotter, 1993; Pink, 2004, 2012; Inglis, 2005; Moran, 2005; Scott, 2009; Smart, 2007; Miller, 2010) the everyday is too readily sidelined within sociology as the study of picayune and mundane *settings* (often so-called private and domestic), in contrast to more extraordinary and heightened situations and forms of experience as found, for example, in religion and the public sphere.

In my view, this dichotomy is misleading. First, it may prevent us from appreciating the admixture of 'special' and routine in all aspects of our lives, whether the mundane and repetitive procedures involved in the doing of science (Latour and Woolgar, 1986 [1979]) or religious devotion (Turner, 2008), or the often-extraordinary features of so-called 'everyday' drudgery (e.g., epiphanous moments while washing the windows; moments of excitement and surprise in scientific work [Garfinkel et al., 1981]). Second, an everyday/extraordinary divide constitutes the everyday as a *place* (e.g., the kitchen, the assembly line, the bus queue) that is associated with a mode of enquiry concerned with cataloguing practices as an end in itself (how the drudgery, say, of doing the laundry is accomplished in this culture versus that one).

While the comparative study of, say, culinary procedures is a fascinating subject, it is not the kind of everyday sociology that I have in mind in what follows. By contrast, I suggest that the everyday can be more fruitfully understood if it is construed conceptually and in ways that capture the temporally charged, often mercurial, equivocal and contingent sense of reality as it is enacted and experienced in the here and now, *wherever* that might be. This conceptualisation means less focus on places and practices as topics in their own right, and more focus on how the enactment of place, practice and meaning actually takes shape.

There are some excellent precedents for this focus in the literature. For example, Pink defines it as 'concerned with treating the performance of practices as lived manifestations of and modifiers of skilled ways of knowing' (2012: 60). In ways that are complementary, Thrift (2008: 12) suggests that we concern ourselves with 'an active and always incomplete incarnation of events, an actualization of times and spaces that uses the fluctuating conditions to assemble itself'.

Thinking about the everyday as practices and processes directs us in turn to the sites within which our (varied and varying) sense of reality is achieved or, as Scott puts it (2009: 1), 'sites in which people do (perform, reproduce, and occasionally challenge) social life, day to day'. Building upon this thought, I reject the idea that there should or could be a sociology 'of' everyday life in the sense that there are sociologies 'of', say, football, food or fashion. By contrast I will suggest that if we consider the everyday conceptually, as the process of accomplishing the 'here and now wherever we are', then the everyday is not an enclave. It cannot, in other words, be abstracted from other social realms and there is nowhere that is not part of everyday life. In short, the everyday is not a set of places or experiences to be contrasted with the extraordinary; it is the site where experience is made manifest, where it takes shape, where sense is made.

In this regard the everyday is the temporal location or 'zero-hour' where realities are brought into being and into focus in ways that matter – to us. The study of this 'hour' involves a rediscovery of the personal in sociology, but not, as Smart observes (2007: 188), in a way that necessarily has to imply individualisation: to the contrary, as we shall see, the sources of the self, the person, identity, relationship, even of individual sensation, stand outside of and are not the personal attributes of any individual.

As I shall describe, this focus on the everyday requires high-resolution methods of investigation. That focus involves detailed, fine-grained engagement with the singular and specific process by which realities came into being – *here*, *this* time, not *there*, *that* time; in *this* place, not in *that* one; through *these* procedures. This concern with singularity or, as Harold Garfinkel (1967) put it, with *haecceity*, is a concern that is shared by scholars working in the field of technology and science studies most notably. It is also a concern that harks back to critical theory and I will explore that matter in Chapter 1 (specifically why Adorno believed that philosophy should consist 'of the qualities it downgrades as contingent, as *quantité négligeable* [negligible quantities]' (2005: 8). And it is a matter of concern within sociological theory today in ways that resonate with pragmatist philosophy. (For example, as the sociologist Randall Collins puts it, '[n]othing has reality unless it is manifested in a situation some-where' [Collins, 2004: 259]. So too, John Dewey's comment that 'things are what they are experienced to be and ... every experience is about some thing' [1934: 247].)

In sum, to be able to trace the short- and longer-term history of expe-rience's production, the assembly of that 'somewhere' (Collins) and 'some thing' (Dewey), is to be able to address the question of how the sense of reality comes to be generated and how it takes shape, albeit contingently and only for a time, *this* way rather than *that* way. This task can be empow-ering, not only for sociologists, but for all of us in our day-to-day lives since it is from within everyday life, and at different moments on a daily basis, that we pose our many questions about 'reality'.

These questions are eclectic and, understandably, often anxious: Am I healthy? Can I be said to have mental capacity? What is my IQ? Are my co-workers trustworthy? Do I look fat in this dress? Am I in danger here? Am I likely to be promoted? Which of them was telling the truth? Is ME a real disease? Will this pain get better? Was that research finding valid? Is she or he really my friend? Is there global warming? Does smoking kill? Is our water clean enough to drink? Does God exist? Is A more beautiful than B? Is violence in this case justified? We may also question where realities come from, how 'solid' they might be, whether some types of reality (physical conditions, natural occurrences, physical laws such as gravity) are more solid than others, or the extent to which different realities are subject to challenge and, therefore, change. While these are philosophically oriented questions, one need not be a philoso-pher to pursue an interest in reality; though, as I will describe in Chapters 1 and 2, philosophers are highly useful in helping us to sharpen the focus on reality.

We are, in short, all reasonably interested in the reality question. It is an existential and ecumenical question, and this point brings me to the question of for whom this book is written. The answer is anyone who has ever wished to contend some claim about what is real (what is good, beautiful, true?) or who has wondered about how it is that things get their realness in the first place. This description includes the non-academic-but-interested reader, budding social scientists and academic professors. Some might object that these groups constitute mutually exclusive readerships; I would disagree for two main reasons. First, 25 years of encounters with students have taught me that: (a) if theory is illustrated with concrete examples it is not necessary to 'dumb it down' for newcomers; (b) no theory is truly useful (or indeed viable) without being grounded in examples; and (c) using grounded examples elaborates theory because it can illuminate matters that we might be unable to anticipate (to that end this book uses many examples: some highly serious and some more deliberately light-hearted). Second, regardless of formal training (indeed, perhaps sometimes in spite of it), we are *all* 'experts' in terms of how we contribute to and account for the making of our worlds.

And so we come to the overall aim of this book. It will take its lead from the quote from Durkheim used as an epigraph for the book. It will take another lead from Goffman, who in his book *Frame Analysis*, and musing on a thought from William James, commented that the crucial question about reality is the one concerned with 'our sense of its realness'. Whether or not something has this quality, Goffman suggests (and here he draws on the analogy of photography), is a problem that has 'to do with the camera and not what it is the camera takes pictures of' (1986 [1977]: 2).

Following these leads, the discussion that follows will develop a perspective devoted to the minute procedures by which our sense of reality takes shape in actual and everyday situations, whether in institutional and organisational settings, in domestic, rural and urban environments, or in online media forums, for all of these locations constitute the settings of our daily experience. This focus will be pursued through three key questions, which further specify the senses in which I use the words *making sense*:

- How is the wide array of what confronts our senses, the so-called sensory manifold, channelled into representations, definitions and claims about reality?
- How do we come to agree upon, and share, these realities and what happens when we do not?
- What are the consequences of different understandings of reality in terms of lost and found opportunities – for the environment, for identities and social relationships?

In addressing these questions, I have two objectives. The first objective is to develop the point that critical attention to world-making processes in everyday life can be interesting, indeed comforting insofar as it helps us to get a grip on the 'why' of how things are (it allows us, as my mother used to say, to 'be philosophical' about things). The second, and more ambitious, objective is to suggest that a perspective devoted to how the sense of reality takes shape can, at least once in a while, help us to change aspects of our worlds and their organisation. Not only do we come to realise that things could be otherwise, but also we can learn how to *create* that otherwise through an understanding of the machinery of reality's production. It seems, therefore, somehow fitting to begin this book by quoting the famous 'thesis eleven' from Karl Marx:

> The philosophers have only interpreted the world, in various ways; the point is to *change* it. (Marx, 1998 [1845]: 571)

Mindful of Marx's exhortation, I have organised into three main parts the nine chapters that follow. Part 1 does a bit of stage-setting with some help from philosophy. In Chapter 1, courtesy of two key philosophers, Ludwig Wittgenstein and Theodor Adorno, I outline the importance of perspectives that value nuanced attention to the things we encounter and which do not presume in advance of these encounters what reality will, or must, be like. Insofar as this perspective puts the brakes on hasty presumptions about reality, it also provides the basis for what I introduce as 'slow sociology' (and I use the term perhaps in a sense that is opposite of Latour's term, 'slowciology' [Latour, 2005: 122]), though I think I am probably otherwise in agreement with his focus on 'tracing' the mutually constitutive connections made between things and people.

My notion of 'slow sociology' takes general inspiration from the 'slow food' culinary movement and the 'slow cinema' movement. It takes more specific inspiration from John Law and his discussion of Appelbaum (1995) and the concept of 'stop' (in which he is considering what can be perceived when 'vision' is produced through the prosthetic of the blind person's stick and the much more tentative movements associated with this form of perception):

> The stop slows us up. It takes longer to do things. It takes longer to understand, to make sense of things. It dissolves the idea, the hope, the belief, that we can see to the horizon, that we can see long distances. It erodes the idea that by taking in the distance at a glance we can get an overview of a single reality. (Law, 2004: 10)

With Chapter 2, I begin to shift tempo, or 'slow things down', by considering the gap between our conventional or received understandings of reality understood as formulations (e.g., natural categories) and the things that they seek to formulate. This is to say that I consider the classification systems (language, scientific categories, images) by which we come to know that which we take to be axiomatic about the world. In particular, I examine the conventional use of dichotomies and binary divides according to which our basic concepts are structured: things such as yes/no, on/off, good/bad, clean/dirty, healthy/ill, pleasant/unpleasant. I suggest that while these dichotomies are useful as devices of ordering (because they require commitments to one or another form of identity and thus provide a series of coordinates for interaction), they are not very useful as empirical descriptors because they over-simplify much subtler matters. This over-simplification can be seen whenever general categories are seen to 'not quite fit' (and thus are partially contradicted by) the singular character of actual instances. As I will describe, those instances can no more determine the shape of general categories than can those categories preordain how their instances will appear on actual occasions. Thus, and in keeping with others who have written on this topic, the complexity of reality is highly resistant to any one neat reality-formulation. Of great interest, therefore, is how this complicated 'mess' gets cleaned up; how formulations come to be made to seem 'realistic' and in ways that lead the eye (or any other sensory modality) away from the gaps between formulations and what they formulate. And for this task we need, as I describe in Part 2, advanced or 'strong' cultural sociology.

To that end, in Part 2, I present the major theoretical themes that form part of a sociology of reality, set up to include a focus on how the sense of reality is achieved. First, in Chapter 3, I review work in cultural sociology devoted to the topic of culturally and technologically mediated or figured reality. Beginning with the famous 'Thomas Theorem' and a focus on the 'definition of the situation', I describe how this definition needs to be fully set in material and institutional contexts in which things – identities, situations – come to be transfigured. A concern with these contexts leads us back to Marx and his emphasis on materiality and material praxis. From there, but retaining the focus on praxis, I consider Durkheim on the symbolic realm leading on into neo-Durkheimian cultural sociology associated with the 'strong programme' today and its concern with how culture is performed.

In Chapter 4 I develop the Durkheimian perspective from, as it were, the 'inside out' by considering the cultural character of the so-called internal realities of embodiment and emotion. That focus includes a concern with how classifications and identifications can inform our experience as we engage in forms of emotional work, and it includes the ways in which cultural and aesthetic media can be seen to 'get into' action through processes of informal learning. These perspectives under-cut any notion of the 'natural' body and turn our attention instead to how embodiment takes shape, which also points out the possibility for cultural variation over time and space.

Chapter 5 considers that variation. I begin with Mary Douglas and the notion of things out of place. I then move on to describe the temporal variability of cultural categories, including micro-temporal variability as culturally mediated conditions shift, wax and wane from second to second. I draw together these themes with a case study of aesthetic-based controversy, one that also addresses head-on the question of things out of place in time, understood as a matter of cultural variability. More substantively, this case study also highlights age-linked presumptions about propriety, ritual grooming, ugliness, and what counts as being 'womanly'.

With Chapter 6 I move into what I consider to be the core of this book and the turning point for the chapters that follow. I consider the question of what kind of reality culture itself is. Referring back to the argument developed in Chapter 2 (the deconstruction or critique of categorical description), I describe how it is misleading to suggest that culture is to be understood simply as a set of background scripts or patterns that in some way come to figure the foreground of action, interaction, agency or experience. By contrast, I focus on how cultural categories (e.g., the categories of femaleness or maleness) are *themselves* matters that have to be realised in situations of action, which is a way of saying that culture ought to be a topic of research, not a resource for sociological explanation. I therefore consider the *mutual alignment of instance and category*. By this I mean that we need to learn how to observe the reflexive relationship between culture, categories, rules and generalities and action, instances, observances and particularities. (For example, who counts as a woman, or a man; how and why; and how that simultaneously constitutes both the person and the category to which they are assigned.) I suggest that this is a core topic for the sociology of reality creation and the point of entry for considering realities as they become manifest in real-time experience. To develop this theme, in Chapter 7, I highlight culture's need for, as it were, realisation in action, examining situations of multiple reality in which the meaning and application of cultural categories are overtly contended. When more than one reality vies for status as the 'real' reality, it is possible to see more clearly how the sense of reality is linked to ways of life and forms of politics, understood in both the experiential and governmental sense.

Having presented the key concepts for understanding reality in terms of *how* it is a creation, I then move into Part 3, where I focus directly on what I describe as the 'artful practices' of reality's enactment. In Chapter 8, building on examples from Wittgenstein, practical magic, neuropsychology, crime fiction and music therapy, I consider the matter of sensing itself, understood as the means and practices by which perception is honed and enhanced (and understood to be inevitably prosthetic). This topic takes us into the very heart of what it means to study the sense of reality, and illuminates perception as a form of action. I suggest that it is possible to trace the 'present history' of how perception and its object can be seen to emerge in relation to situations that enhance perception. I also detail the minute practices that are often glossed over when we speak, more generically, of perception. Through that detailing, I will aim to contribute to a growing concern in the scholarly literatures with pre-cognitive ways of knowing (what are we conscious of 'knowing', what do we 'know' without knowing we know it, and which forms of knowing/sensing come to be hailed as 'the' ways of knowing the world?). It is there, I suggest, that we can learn from the realm of magic and conjuring, in terms of how perception can be directed and how that process itself can tell us about how culture gets into action. This learning in turn helps us to see how realities should be understood as 'virtually real'.

In Chapter 9, I return to the question of how the sense of reality is achieved, this time in order to showcase the importance of mundane, devoted and recurrent action as the engine of that process. I ask the following question: how is it possible that people manage to create virtually real realities despite – as is often the case – confusion, disorganisation, multiple orientations, ambiguity and time pressure such that the possibility of seemingly mutual situations of human contact are made possible? I then develop what I think may be the most important lesson of this book, that realities are virtually real but nonetheless real in their consequences. To underline this point I use examples dealing with the situated enactment of ability/disability and capacity/incapacity. I suggest that these, often-medicalised, realities can be seen to emerge according to how social situations are arranged. By way of conclusion, I suggest that these examples show perhaps more clearly than any others how ecologies of action/perception distribute opportunities and possibilities for being and acting in the world. I suggest that we need, therefore, to consider carefully what kinds of sense it is possible to make.

PART 1

PHILOSOPHICALLY INFORMED SOCIOLOGY

1

INTRODUCING SLOW SOCIOLOGY

Thinking about how our senses of reality take shape in daily life involves both general and specific questions. The general questions will be familiar to philosophers. They include matters such as: What is 'the world'? How solid are realities within the world? What does it take to effect change in the nature of reality? Is reality embedded 'in' things, or does it reside 'in' the relations between things? To what extent is reality an outcome of cultural practice? How do we come to know realities? What is the relationship between knowing realities and the realities we know?

To pose these questions is in turn to ask about the *flexibility* of realities, namely: to what extent can reality *change its shape* as it passes from place to place, time to time, perceiver to perceiver and situation to situation? And what kind of relationship is there between our assumptions about (and practices toward) realities and the forms that those realities appear to take? These are general questions but they can be made more specific through worked examples. For example, we can investigate specific situations where realities come to be taken as real, where they are initially experienced as real, and where, once realised, they have consequences for the making of other realities. In this chapter I describe how a focus on these matters requires a painstakingly close form of attention associated with what I will call 'Slow Sociology'.

I call this form of sociology 'slow' because, metaphorically and sometimes literally, it requires a form of attention to minutiae. This attention is akin to the slow motion, wide-lens, long-take techniques associated with 'slow cinema' and with the comparatively time-consuming methods associated with producing and preparing 'slow food'. These techniques – cognitive and empirical but also aesthetic and sensory – are devoted to the cultivation of intimate forms of knowledge and to the detailed features of what happens locally, here and now; and they have an affinity with ethnographic forms of enquiry (Atkinson et al., 2001), and the focus on embodied craft (Atkinson, 2013) and on the skills involved in living together (Sennett, 2008, 2012). Slow sociology is, in other words, an anti-generic mode of enquiry focused on the particularities of things, rather than the more general and often hypothetical (or indeed metaphysical) there and then. It is perhaps akin to what Goethe knew as 'gentle empiricism', ways of being with the world and learning through unobtrusive observation (see Ansdell and Pavlicevic, 2010), beautifully enunciated by Fox Keller, in her study of the Nobel laureate and cytogeneticist, Barbara McClintock:

> 'No two plants are exactly alike. They're all different, and as a consequence, you have to know that difference,' she [McClintock] explains. 'I start with the seedling, and I don't want to leave it. I don't feel I really know the story if I don't watch the plant all the way along. So I know every plant in the field. I know them intimately, and I find it a great pleasure to know them.'

> This intimate knowledge, made possible by years of close association with the organism she studies, is a prerequisite for her extraordinary perspicacity ... Both literally and figuratively, her 'feeling for the organism' has extended her vision ... (Fox Keller, 1983: 198)

Slow sociology can, I shall suggest, inhibit our sometimes too-hasty assumptions about the realities that we believe 'must' exist – in society, nature or ourselves (e.g., 'It was like that then, there, so it must be like that now, here'). Taking it slow helps us to consider the moments and devices – linguistic but also enacted through materials (documents, objects, technologies) and forms of embodiment – that sever realities from their histories of production (their origins and growth). Understanding the provenance of realities, whether over the long term or short term, is, as I shall describe, a way of preserving the possibility for critique, for challenging assertions about what is real. (As Inglis [2013: 15] observes, '[a]s Orwell knew, how we think about ourselves and our future is utterly dependent on how we imagine the past'.)

This historically informed understanding includes an understanding of how our idiomatic styles and languages for thinking about ontology, or the nature of reality, themselves have histories, and of how they have been modified over time. (For example, Pollner [1987] has described how the idea of a 'real' and an 'objective' world can be traced within the history of philosophy and science.) It also includes, as we shall see, a concern with the provenance of the objects, materials and tools (MacKenzie and Wajcman, 1999 [1985]; Norman, 2002 [1988]; Bijker et al., 1989), since our material agency takes shape in relation to, and through the media of, these things – as Pickering puts it, a dance or 'dialectic of resistance and accommodation' (Pickering, 1995: 21–2, 52). Step by step, this 'dance' has consequences, as Molotch explains:

How we desire, produce, and discard the durables of existence helps form who we are, how we connect to one another, and what we do to the earth. In addition to ordering intimacies, these urges and actions influence the way peoples across large stretches of time, cultures, and geographies align, exchange, and conflict. (Molotch, 2005: xi)

Thus slow sociology is a perspective and a set of methods devoted to recovering the present history of how things 'are' and how our sense of how things are is made, through practices and in relation to, as Molotch calls them, 'the durables of existence'. It is an often-painstakingly detailed form of enquiry that seeks to avoid any jumping to conclusions about how reality 'just is' or 'must be'.

WITTGENSTEIN ON 'MUST'

As a way into what 'more slow' (Marvel, n.d. [*c.* 1650]) forms of enquiry can offer, consider how we come to use the expression 'it must be' and how this expression can lead us to over-assert that which can be known. The philosopher Ludwig Wittgenstein is helpful on this point.

As Pleasant puts it (1999: 40, quoting Wittgenstein), '"must"', that means we are going to apply this picture come what may' (Wittgenstein, 1976: 411, quoted in Pleasants, 1999: 40). By contrast, Wittgenstein advises against situations in which we cleave to 'preconceived idea[s] to which reality *must* correspond' (Wittgenstein, 1968: 131, quoted in Pleasants, 1999: 40). As Pleasants notes, Wittgenstein believes we can do better, that we '*look and see* ... don't think, but look!' (p. 122), advocating an open-minded attitude toward reality, 'rather than deciding *a priori*, on the basis of an ontological picture of how things *must*, and can only be' (p. 122). In other words, our theoretical preconceptions about how reality 'must' look run the risk of being overly selective and thus can lead us to impose presumptions about reality on the particular instances of what we remember about the past, and what we encounter and perceive in the present. These preconceptions may excise richer and more sensorial, pre-cognitive dimensions of knowing and remembering and the intimate knowledge associated with these dimensions. While I do not mean to imply that there is a 'purer' or 'better' way of knowing the world that can be achieved if only we overthrow the 'blinders' of conventional categories of perception ('presumptions' versus 'perceptions'), I do mean to suggest that each and every set of preconceptions about reality enacts selective processes of knowing and remembering. The question then is what, as a result of preconceptions, is gained, and what is lost. What, in other words, is retained as the memory (or relatively fixed idea) of what is, and is not, real?

On memory, the cognitive sociologist Aaron Cicourel (1974) has described how the human mind can only process so much 'on line', as Saferstein puts it (Saferstein, 2010: 115), in any given moment. Our remembrance of things is, Cicourel suggests, dependent upon things external to the mind, such as objects, tools and aesthetic media which frame and elicit selective memories (e.g., when I smell that perfume I remember my mother; when I hear this song I am transported 'back then'). (In this respect Cicourel's work presaged the extended mind perspective in philosophy [Clark and Chalmers, 1998] and the focus on distributed cognition in anthropology [Hutchins, 1995]. It also complements and has informed work on memory artefacts, for example in relation to the representational politics of collective memory [Tota, 2004, 2005] and to self-remembrance [DeNora, 2000].)

On encountering and perceiving aspects of the world, our belief or pre-commitments to what we expect to encounter may excise, or filter out, those things that we do not expect to encounter or which 'really should not be there'. These, at times, incorrigible beliefs may lead us to witness things that were not actually there, and *not* to witness things that are there. Psychologists speak of this filtering as 'inattentional blindness' (Mack and Rock, 1998; Simons and Chabris, 1999). This form of 'blindness' occurs when our expectations of what we should or must see actually prevent us from noticing things that do not square with our presumptions of what must or must not be, to return to Wittgenstein's words, in 'this picture'.

The most famous example used to illustrate inattentional blindness involves an experiment where subjects were asked to view a basketball game in which team members were dressed, contrastingly, in black and white shirts (Simons and Chabris, 1999). The experimental subjects were asked to count how many times the basketball was passed between white-shirted players. During the game, a gorilla-suited figure walked through the court, pausing briefly (see Figure 1.1). Most subjects never noticed the gorilla because they were so intent upon the assigned perceptual task. They were not, in other words, looking for a gorilla and they therefore did not, on the whole, notice a gorilla. The example highlights how at times matters that are literally, in this case, in centre court, can pass unnoticed because of the ways in which attention is selectively devoted to its object. Equally importantly, this experiment showed how attention can be directed and framed (in this case the task and instructions of how to watch), a topic to which we will return in Chapter 8.

While the matter of seeing a gorilla-suited figure in a contrived experiment may seem trivial, other matters of perception and what perception does and does not permit us to sense and know may be more

©1999 Daniel Simons. All rights reserved.

Figure 1.1 Gorillas in our midst: Sustained inattentional blindness for dynamic events (Simons and Chabris, 1999). Figure provided by Daniel Simons. See also: http://www.dansimons.com

serious, as we shall explore momentarily and throughout this book. For now, the example of inattentional blindness helps to highlight why Wittgenstein advised us to '*look and see … don't think but look!*' The trouble with this advice is that looking and thinking are not ultimately separate activities. (As I will discuss much later in Chapter 8, looking and thinking are interrelated and mutually constituting and they are always social activities.) To the contrary: careful, inclusive looking is aided by forms of thinking, or, more broadly, representing, forms that can widen – or narrow – the lens, sensitising us to what is 'in the frame' (what there is to know, experience, do). In so doing, they widen the window or span of conscious attention, *quantitatively*, in terms of the time held in short-term memory, and *qualitatively*, in terms of what is noticed. Jumping to conclusions ('it must be so'), along with over-socialised, over-intent or narrow-focus forms of perception (versus the so-called 'soft eyes' or wider-angle focus that looks but does not stare), can deflect attention from more nuanced appreciation of what there is to know ('what else could this be?').

More insidiously, this kind of haste may push us into forms of categorical, generic thinking that lead to cognitive violence (not doing justice to the phenomena) and which at times may in turn lead on to forms of physical violence and oppression. On this point it is time to introduce a second key thinker who, while not fully aligned with the perspectives I will be developing, nonetheless helps to establish the project of 'slow' sociology. I refer to the critical theorist Theodor W. Adorno.

ADORNO ON FORM AND CONTENT, OPPRESSION AND CRITIQUE

Adorno's work was devoted to illuminating how we fail to notice that which contradicts our (often implicit) assumptions about reality. Adorno was concerned to show how reality is not reducible to or identical with the concepts by which we seek to know it. Conceptualisation, classification and categorisation, therefore, left what Adorno called 'a remainder' (Adorno, 2005: 5) – aspects or parts of phenomena that do not fit into the shape and terms of the common denominator, or descriptor. For Adorno, the challenge of social life was to achieve a (temporary and always shifting) balance between subject and object, particular and general, so as to minimise the violence (both symbolic and real) of remaindering. This task, Adorno believed, required nuanced attention to detail and a feeling for multiplicity and equivocality.

In Adorno's understanding, one of the most dangerous features of thought was its tendency to be overly generic. As a half-Jewish philosopher working during the early part of his career in Germany during National Socialism, Adorno witnessed first hand the consequences of categorical thinking: the dangers of believing that the contents of the social world were 'really' aligned with the forms that we use to describe and know that world. This is to say that Adorno considered that totalitarian regimes of all kinds buttressed forms of persecution with notions that people could be easily classified into types. Under National Socialism, these 'types' were in turn ranked such that Jews, Slavs, homosexuals, women [*sic* – I use the regime's categorical descriptions] were deemed inferior and/or unworthy of full human rights. These malicious, hasty understandings laid the cognitive foundation, Adorno considered, for behavioural cruelty.

By contrast, Adorno valued modes of understanding that facilitated the perception of difference. The recognition of difference, which is to say the recognition of the 'non-identity' between an assumption of what a category 'must' contain and what is actually encountered in specific instances (e.g., 'My goodness but aren't you strong/intelligent for a woman/child/old person/blond-haired person!'), was a way of accommodating a richer and more nuanced, variegated, complicated and surprising reality. That accommodation was one concerned with formal innovation, with finding formal containers that could 'hold' more of reality's contradictions and so stretch the span of what could be held within consciousness (as discussed above in relation to thinking and looking). That kind of cognitive capaciousness was, Adorno considered, also the basis for tolerance.

To return to the parallel with the 'slow' movements and further illustrate the point that categories selectively represent reality and may structure perception and evaluation, let's now consider a different example (albeit one that is as simple as it is less urgent). Consider the case of a category of fruit – the tomato, for example. At different times in the history of food in Europe, the tomato was (a) unknown, (b) considered potentially poisonous and thus not a food source, and (c) a staple salad or sauce ingredient. In recent times, the slow food and organic food movements have sought to remind us that not all tomatoes are round and red, or how, in some cases, a tomato might be more like a physalis or even a grape. Now think of all the tomatoes that would be 'remaindered' (and thus wasted) if we used the image of the red, round one as the common denominator of 'tomato-ness'. So too with slow cognition, or ways of accommodating a wider array of things that might not otherwise 'fit' into conventional containers of how reality 'must' be, or look:

> *Horatio:* O day and night, but this is wondrous strange!
>
> *Hamlet:* And therefore as a stranger give it welcome. There are more things in heaven and earth, Horatio, Than are dreamt of in your philosophy (Shakespeare, *Hamlet*, Act 1, Scene 5)

FORM AND CONTENT, KNOWING AS COMPOSING

It is probably not fruitful to speculate on whether Adorno would have endorsed the slow or organic food movements (Adorno's negative hauteur tended to lead him to disapprove of all popular movements). Nonetheless, the point of describing the tomato and its vicissitudes highlights a matter close to the heart of Adorno's philosophy – the relation between form and content. Adorno was concerned with how overly simplistic forms could trick perception, leading us into too-hasty identifications between instances and categories (e.g., 'this is not a tomato') and – the next move in the game – the danger associated with too-hasty thinking: the ease of moving from 'it must be this' to 'we must do this'.

This philosophy of form was linked to his more general concern with reality's composition or with how specific materials come to be assembled into socially recognisable, conventional forms that can be or are posited as requiring to be shared or known between people (Witkin,

1998; DeNora, 2003). In this regard, Adorno's thinking about composition was in turn linked to, and greatly influenced by, his second professional pursuit, that of musician and composer. It is interesting to follow Adorno's theory of culture, in particular his notion of aesthetic form as an active ingredient of sense-making (a point that will be critical later on, in Part 2, when we consider 'strong' forms of cultural sociology today). And so we come to the first of this book's case study examples.

CASE STUDY   Adorno on 'composition'

For Adorno, musical composition, understood as the arrangement of sound, or sonic material, was important for two reasons. First, musical composition (or at least Adorno's own understanding of composition) offered a metaphor or exemplar for cognition. Second, Adorno considered that composition provided an active condition of consciousness (cognition, perception, awareness) and its formation. While one might dispute the ways in which Adorno drew connections between musical genre, composers and styles and their actual uses and interpretations, and indeed question whether Adorno paid sufficient attention to popular musical forms (Witkin, 2000; DeNora, 2003; Rojek, 2011), his work is invaluable for cultural sociology because it develops a theory of how aesthetic materials 'get into' our processes of thought and attention to the world.

As a metaphor or exemplar for consciousness and knowledge production (or knowledge 'composition'), Adorno understood compositional practices to model the ways that difference in other, extra-musical realms could be handled or accommodated. For example, consider the standard pop-ballad love song. Setting aside the question of its lyrics and focusing only on its arrangement of tonal material, the ballad employs a harmonic arrangement that prioritises melody (one voice) over the potential for equal voices. It requires a 'type' of ending, such as a musical climax or a fade-out. It also places certain constraints upon singers, such as that the pitch of the voice 'must' be in tune, and they 'must' be rhythmically entrained and in tempo, or the singer risks being deemed inept (e.g., not worthy of a record contract, an audience, etc.). So the composer 'must' be committed to these conventions if she or he is to be a writer of pop songs, as certain harmonic, melodic and rhythmic arrangements will not be tolerated. By contrast, a composer may attempt to work in forms that admit more of the irregular, misshapen, deformed or, as he puts it in relation to modern ('serious') music which took upon itself, 'all the darkness and guilt of the world. Its fortune lies in the perception of misfortune; all of its beauty is in denying itself the illusion of beauty' (Adorno, 1980: 133).

Thus, for Adorno, an over-adherence to pre-given forms involved characteristic practices of handling material, and these practices called for the editing-out of some forms of sonic difference (rejecting 'deformed' material). Because not all sonic material could be accommodated by pre-given, overly familiar forms, those forms could be read, metaphorically, as object lessons in intolerance and, by contrast, less conventional forms as object lessons in how to maintain a delicate empirical 'respect' for those things that did not readily 'fit' into conventional forms. The analogy to food – and the slow food movement – is again apt: just as some supermarkets may remainder or dispose of 'misshapen' tomatoes, so too some compositional practices refused, and therefore were unaccommodating to, 'misshapen' sounds.

But for Adorno music was more than a metaphor. It was also a condition of consciousness and, as such, Adorno conceived of music as a medium by which attentive capacities (the span of consciousness) could be enhanced or diminished. More specifically, forms that admitted the sonically strange or deformed, that found ways of accommodating sonic difference, were forms that could stretch perceptual and cognitive faculties to admit greater nuance, contradiction and rival possibilities. By contrast, highly familiar, predictable forms were the comfort food of the ears, reinforcing simple habits of mind in ways that relaxed the tension required for differentiation. They were associated, Adorno believed, with a 'regression in hearing' that led listeners into forgetfulness of the potentially wider realm of sonic possibility and thus to other possible orientations to the world (including sensibilities). So, to continue with the food analogy, overly familiar, clichéd musical concoctions could, Adorno considered, dull the sense of hearing so that discernment, the ability to *really listen* (recall Wittgenstein above on 'looking'), was suppressed.

To return to the example of tomatoes: the clichéd notion is that a tomato 'must' be round and red, as opposed, say, to the subtle and slightly furry texture of a freshly picked, outdoor-grown, deliberately under-watered Cherokee Purple (Hudson, 2013) or the 'deformed' tomato that is shaped like a nose, or half-nibbled by another animal but picked and eaten anyway. Or think about the taste, smell and texture of a freshly picked tomato, or one that has not been kept under refrigeration as it travels far afield. (For a similar discussion, see Thoreau, 1986 [1854]: 220, on the huckleberry: '[i]t is a vulgar error to suppose that you have tasted huckleberries who never plucked them … The ambrosial and essential part of the fruit is lost with the bloom which is rubbed off in the market cart, and they become mere provender.') Only musical forms that sought to accommodate the 'strangeness' or

(Continued)

(Continued)

'simultaneous multiplicity' of material (what it was and was not, what it could do, how it sounded) were enriching.

For Adorno, this accommodation involved a dialectical or mutually interactive relationship between form and content. This is to say that while Adorno valued forms that were inclusive of material's diversity, he also valued form, which he understood as socially recognisable and shared ways of containing material. Therefore, and unlike some more 'experimental' composers, such as John Cage, Adorno did not advocate opening up the world of sounds to their fully anarchic possibilities, for example, in ways that would allow 'raw' sound to be classed as 'music', as in Cage's so-called 'silent' piece, 4'33" (where the 'music' is the ambient sound of the location where it is performed, filling the time interval of 4 minutes and 33 seconds). Nor did Adorno value more deterministic methods of composition (where material was arranged according to pre-fixed formulae [see DeNora, 2011: Ch. 1]). Thus, 'composition' had to negotiate between two extremes: on the one hand, if music upheld form over content, it collapsed its potential to present difference; its compass became too narrow. On the other hand, if music allowed sonic content free-rein, the possibility for sharing meaningful forms was missed and with it the importance of musical form as a model or exemplar for collective being. ('Music says We directly, regardless of its intentions' [Adorno, 1997: 167].)

As we shall see, the fitting-together of form and content, general and particular, part and whole, is the work of reality's composition. The study of this composition should, as I have suggested, proceed slowly; and the forms that composition takes, that is, actors' renditions of realities and our accounts of these renditions, when they are tailored to accommodate diverse material, may not bear resemblance to our presuppositions of how they 'must' take shape. Thus, and taking our cue from Adorno on composition, a 'slow' approach is one that tries to admit more into the picture, that allows for greater degrees of possibility and potential, and that therefore risks (indeed courts or flirts with) confusion and uncertainty.

This uncertainty in turn provides some distance from the common-sense understanding of reality and the idea that reality is, as John Law describes (Law, 2004: 23–7) in his five-point summary: (1) 'out there', (2) independent of our actions and our perceptions, (3) standing before or preceding us, (4) definite and (5) singular (i.e., not competing with other versions of the real). And, as I will describe in Chapter 2, while looking and thinking cannot be neatly severed from each other (they are mutually constitutive), we may nonetheless take a step toward looking for and thinking about that which does not seek to impose a preconceived pattern, one that is interested in what is different, incoherent and, in Law's terms, messy. From there, it is possible to take another step into that mess by acknowledging that the patterns which we perceive are patterns that we ourselves are complicit in assembling, through active perception and through the assembly or furbishing of situations conducive to these perceptions. As we move toward that complexity, we are also moving toward an understanding of reality as open-ended, and toward an understanding of knowing the world as a form of critical praxis. Within those understandings, composed realities are revealed as places and spaces – ecologies – for being in the world.

2

CONVENTIONAL AND UNCONVENTIONAL REALITIES: THE CASE OF SEXUAL DIFFERENCE

As a starting point for this praxis, consider how seemingly 'real' differences between types of people or things can be called into question, and in ways that undercut over-hasty presumptions about difference and similarity. This calling into question in turn highlights the tension between form and content with which Adorno was concerned; how to create categories capable of holding as much difference as possible (Adorno's 'remainders') while also facilitating shared realities. To develop this discussion, I will consider one of the most basic, binary forms of human/animal difference that we often take for granted – the difference between men and women, biologically speaking.

The male/female dichotomy shows quite clearly the ways in which form (male versus female) and content (particular instances of physiology, anatomy and physique as found in individual people) exist in mutual tension. To develop this discussion I will begin with a fairly light-hearted example of this mutual tension between form and content and then I will turn to more consequential, and more complicated, examples.

A CHILD'S GUIDE TO THE DIFFERENCE BETWEEN BOYS AND GIRLS

Men, we might assert, are taller than women. Imagine then the surprise that a childish mind might express when it comes across a counter-example (think of Tom Cruise standing next to Nicole Kidman). The childish (overly hasty) mind eventually learns that the notion of men being taller is 'only' a general notion (it refers only to the class or category 'men'): it is not an absolute feature to which all men 'must' conform (one can be a man without being tall!). Form and content are not, in other words, identical.

Logicians might suggest that this childish understanding asserts a faulty version of a standard-form categorical proposition. Such a proposition goes like this: 'Tom is a man. All men are taller than women. Tom must be taller than Nicole.' The proposition asserts that all members or subjects of a predicate term or class (men, in this case) will be/have X characteristic (be taller than women in this case) and that, assuming Tom is a man, then he 'must' be taller than all women, and therefore he 'must' be taller than Nicole. The problem here is that the argument contains a false premise – *not* all men are taller than all women. Simple, and somewhat absurd as it may seem, this example allows for two important matters to be noted, both of which help to illuminate what we do when we make realities such as these in daily life. First, the categorical proposition is, as logicians have observed, 'important … because many of the statements we make in ordinary discourse are either categorical propositions as they stand or are readily translatable into them' (Hurley, 2008: 190). Second, and given the ubiquity of categorical propositions in everyday life, it is worth paying close attention to those things that are deemed to be premises (forms, or containers of reality) and to reflect critically upon the ways that premises may structure our ability to perceive in nuanced ways ('don't think but look').

So, to continue with the example of sexual difference, we know from practical experience that the reality of categorical differences in height between men and women is more complicated, that the binary division is not an absolute but a generality with many exceptions, Tom and Nicole being a case in point. As Lynda Birke (1992b) has described it, the binary categories of biological sex – male versus female – are too simple; there are intra-categorical differences (differences between men, differences between women) that are sometimes greater than the inter-categorical differences (differences between men and women), one of the more obvious being height. (We will consider some of the less obvious examples later.) At the same time, the general idea (most men are taller than most women) may colour how we behave toward, and evaluate, individual men and women and in ways that are compelling and consequential. I will describe now three interrelated sets of questions linked to these points – the cultural inflection of our categories of difference, the suppression of intra-categorical difference, and the consequences that are attendant on categorical notions of reality.

INSTANCES AND CATEGORIES, OR
ONTOLOGIES AND THEIR CONSEQUENCES

First, and sticking with the example of sexual difference, general understandings of biological differences can become easily inflected with cultural assumptions and values (indeed, as we shall see shortly, they *are* cultural assumptions and values). For example, the general assumption that men are taller than women may lead to further assumptions that shorter men exhibit (and note the discourse here) 'lack of height', or that taller women exhibit 'excessive height'. And yet, these judgements involve circular thinking; tallness in women, or shortness in men, is only problematic if we determine that height is a key or primary characteristic of something valuable, if it is coupled to things that are distinct from height, if there is some reason (past or present, aesthetic, practical, biological, social) why it is 'important' for men to be taller than women. Our understanding of the (as we may call them) 'natural differences' between men and women, in other words, is easily tainted by our cultural and perhaps emotionally inflected understandings of the differences between manliness and womanliness, and in ways that may reverse-engineer how we perceive difference, perceiving the actual differences as somehow 'going against' our presumed understandings of how the picture 'ought' to look (recall Wittgenstein's words, 'we are going to apply this picture come what may'). Conceptions of 'natural' sexual difference become easily meshed with conceptions of *meaningful*, cultural differences.

Second, and once we see how assumptions about the natural world are entwined with cultural assumptions, we may ask about how the borders between things (e.g., between men and women and both individual men/women and collectives of men/women) are secured through social, technical and aesthetic practices that involve the clustering-together of different types of meaningful differences (men are taller and they also have more prominent chins along with facial hair), and that involve operations upon the natural world so as to help it to 'look like' it 'must' or 'ought' to do. So, for example, a man/men might worry about being 'too short' or a woman/women about being 'too tall'. To 'compensate', a man/men might opt for elevator shoes to 'gain height' (while a woman/women might stoop and wear flat-healed shoes so as not to 'tower over' men). Or a man (or whole groups of men) might be worried about having a 'weak chin' (or a woman/women might worry about too prominent a chin). And to 'compensate', a man/men might employ a beard (while a woman/women might be able to manage to hide a protruding chin with a 'clever' haircut). These 'compensations' (modifications) can accumulate over the long term such that we begin

to assume that they are 'just natural', axiomatic. (For example, generations of men and women engaged in practices so as to make themselves
into men and women; so too, they have, across different cultures, engaged
in patterns of physical work that lay down muscular-skeletal forms of
sex/gender differentiation.) As Birke observes (1992a: 75):

> What you are now – your biological body – is a product of com-
> plex transformations between biology and experiences in your
> past. And these transformations happening now will affect any such
> transformations in the future. Biology, in this view, does have a role:
> but it is neither a base to build on nor determining.

Birke describes here how we cannot claim to find even biological realities 'in' nature, but rather that differences, even physical biological ones,
can be better understood to take shape through nature/culture practices.
As Scott and Jackson (quoting Crossley, 2001) note (2010: 147), bodies:

> are classified from birth and even before' and 'this process of cate-
> gorization ... effects a "social magic" ' ... This 'marking' of bodies
> is not simply symbolic – investing them with signifiers of, for
> example, class, gender and ethnicity – but also material, in that
> social location and biographical events leave physical traces on
> bodies (e.g. effects of diet, environment, physical and emotional
> labour: Morgan and Scott, 1993) as well as endowing us with a
> particular bodily hexis (Bourdieu, 1992). (Crossley, 2001: 147)

I will return to these issues in Chapter 3 ('*Performing* femininity') and
also below (see 'Nobody's perfect').

Third, we may ask about how opportunities for category membership
come to be distributed according to the ways that categories come to be
defined and linked to adjacent categories such as gender identities and
their associated opportunities for action. So, for example, is it more difficult to count as 'feminine' if one is seven feet tall? If one has, like the
artist Frida Kahlo, a slight moustache? If one is fat? Old? Gray (see
Chapters 5 and 6)? 'Disabled' [*sic*] in some way (I will return to the word
'disabled' in Chapter 9)? And finally, we may ask about the politics of
category formation, the 'who, where, when and how' of cultural innovation, stabilisation and change, a topic I discuss in Chapter 6.

The example I have just used of sexual and gender differences highlights once again Adorno's emphasis on the importance of being able to
recognise difference, to note the ways in which form and content are
not identical (not all men are [list criteria A, B, C ...]). To speak of this
recognition is to speak of anti-discriminatory forms of cognition, a
habit of mind that is able to note difference and that does not assume

all instances 'must' conform to a generic pattern. Continuing with the example of sex/gender difference, in particular how gendered notions affect our assumptions about how nature ought to look, let's now pursue that point through a seemingly mundane example, the case of body hair and its varyingly problematic status within situations of daily life. (Recall Adorno on how forms admit greater or lesser degrees of material, and now consider how the formal category 'woman' is selective about what it admits, and refuses to admit, within its auspices, thereby constraining how we perceive that which is womanly and that which is not.) How accommodating are our categories of reality and what sacrifices do they require? What will they not admit? Addressing this question involves, as we shall see, a sociology of the aspects of things that get removed, hidden or suppressed (remaindered) so that reality comes to look like 'reality', to accord with, in Wittgenstein's sense, the 'picture' of what 'must' be. That investigation in turn highlights how the personal is political and thus connects with C. Wright Mills' famous concern with sociology as a mode of understanding that transforms, conceptually, individuals' personal uneasiness or troubles into 'involvement with public issues' (Mills, 2000 [1959]: 5). We will consider that matter now in relation to gender and grooming rituals, specifically the presence or absence of body hair.

CASE STUDY   Unwanted hair, or unwanted dichotomies? A two-part tale

Part One (narrative story, anonymised source)

As a woman in my early twenties [says Maria], I lived for a time in what I and my housemates described (in aspirational terms) as an alternative, feminist, perhaps social anarchist household. This household was in turn linked to lots of other things we did and valued, like belonging to a coop, vegetarianism, anti-consumerism as we then saw it, and, to a very limited extent on my part, political activism. Thinking back on all this now, 30 years later, I realise now how these values were a bit inconsistent. [Author's note: the issue of what cultural consistency is or is not will be considered in Chapter 6.]

As part of my commitment to this lifestyle, I valued what I thought were 'natural' forms of femininity (no chemicals, low maintenance, independence from the beauty industry). To that

(Continued)

(Continued)

end, I stopped shaving my legs. For some of my friends, this practice was no big deal. But then they did not have dark hair. Eventually, the hair grew in and, as expected, my legs looked unambiguously 'hairy', visible to the casual glance, and even, as it turned out, visibly hairy from some distance [read on].

At first I felt brave, in defiance of, as I saw it, compulsory, femininity. As time passed, I simply got used to the hair and forgot about it. Then one day during the summer, when I was walking down the street wearing a knee-length skirt (muslin, elephant-patterned, wrap-around), a car full of young men drove by and one of them leaned out the window and shouted (and the shouting-out at me was itself slightly startling), 'Shave your legs!'

Later that same summer, I went to see my parents. My mom belonged to a swim club. This was emphatically not a country club but a glorious old, shabby, artesian-spring-fed pool, inexpensive and not exclusive, a family venue. We would sit in the somewhat rickety lounge chairs, swim, read, eat hot dogs, chat and nap. It was a highly sociable environment and I lament its passing.

While the ethos of the club could be described as laid back – the owners were almost bohemian in some ways – the club hadn't yet come to grips with or embraced such things as whole food vegetarianism, radical feminism, or social anarchist agendas (one might ask, 'Why ever should they?').

The day before what would be my first visit of the summer to this club, my mother asked me in the nicest possible way if I might consider shaving my legs. It was not that she 'minded' (she would still love me!) but that the legs could possibly be read as impolite, a kind of affront, even a form of disrespect. And the group of ladies we sat with were old friends, women who were in their late fifties and early sixties who'd known me since I was a little girl.

And so I shaved my legs. I did not want to 'force' an issue with my mother (and besides, I told myself, my values and ethics hinged upon more than a few hairs!). I did not want to make old friends uncomfortable. But also, in this swimming club world, the hair didn't make sense; it seemed to contradict what that world *felt* like, what being, and looking like, 'a woman' in that world consisted of. So, while I was 'conforming' (giving in), I was also trying to be in tune with the spirit of the place as a club member. And anyway, as for my previous commitments, well, I knew that hair would grow back, indeed perhaps more lavishly than ever.

Part Two

The issue of hair in the wrong place (increasingly for men as well as women; witness men's waxing salons) is alive and well. For example, a July 2012 issue of *The Metro* (a free newspaper often found at public transport sites such as Tube and rail stations in the UK) reported on actress Pixie Lott who appeared in public with visible hair growth under her arms ('The hairy armpit moment'). As *The Metro* observed, the 'same mistake' (of appearing in public with hairy armpits) was made in 1999 by actress Julia Roberts. The article went on to suggest that Lott should have learned her lesson ('the cardinal rules') and taken advantage of the wide range of grooming products so that 'the tiny black hairs' could have been eradicated.

The case of body hair illustrates how different groups articulate particular versions of sexual/gender difference through images of what biological reality looks like (women do/do not have body hair) and how they attempt to secure different renditions of what that reality 'must' look like. The seemingly trivial cases I have just described (Maria's narrative; the *Metro* story) show us how biological notions (the meshing-together of what female bodies 'must' look like with what particular bodies 'should' look like) are employed and enhanced by reference to normative, cultural notions (what women's bodies 'ought to' look like). This admixture of discourses – the natural and the normative – is in turn related to the practices by which we handle natural material (body hair in this case). In shaving the hair we are aligning the body with 'the picture' of what that body 'must' look like if it is an instance of the category 'women' (remember Wittgenstein on how 'we are going to apply this picture come what may'). (The 'remainder' of this process – the shaven hairs – are disposed of down the drain.) In not shaving the hair we are breaching this picture, calling the viewer's attention to how the categorical, either/or proposition (women have no body hair/men have body hair) is false.

The example of hair (unwanted/wanted) is therefore useful for illustrating how categories of reality in everyday life, even including notions of the so-called 'natural', are *dynamic*: they have living histories; they are problematic; they are potentially always in flux, always contestable, and always tied to ways of life, to ethics and aesthetics. Thus, the example also highlights just how much is at stake when we 'forget' that women have hair. It is not the hair that should be 'unwanted' but the either/or proposition that women have no body hair while men do have body hair. The next example highlights how there is even more at stake when we forget that the two-sex world is by no means ordained ('wanted') by biology.

CASE STUDY 'Nobody's perfect' – Fausto-Sterling on 'the five sexes'

In an article with the subtitle 'Why Male and Female Are Not Enough', Anne Fausto-Sterling describes how, as she puts it, 'Western culture is deeply committed to the idea that there are only two sexes.' Fausto-Sterling goes on to outline how this sexual dichotomy is embedded in language ('his and hers'), in law (draft registration, voting rights, marriage and laws that regulate sexual conduct), the workplace and, of course, custom (fashion, leisure pursuits, grooming rituals such as hair removal). And yet, as Fausto-Sterling (herself a trained biologist) puts it, 'biologically speaking, there are many gradations running from female to male and depending on how one calls the shots, one can argue that along that spectrum lie at least five sexes – and perhaps even more' (1993: 20). The confusion is sufficient, as Fausto-Sterling suggests, to defy the 'reality' of a two-sex world. Fausto-Sterling goes on to describe how the 'two-sexed' world can be re-specified in terms of different categories of intersex, male hermaphrodites ('one testis and one ovary'), pseudohermaphrodites ('testes and some aspects of female genitalia but no ovaries') and female pseudohermaphrodites ('who have ovaries and some aspects of the male genitalia but lack testes'). She describes how even these categories exhibit considerable intra-categorical variation. And then she suggests that we consider redefining the binary sexual classification scheme so that it will allow for five, rather than two, biological sexes.

As Fausto-Sterling describes, naturally occurring sexual diversity is mostly erased through medical techniques of hormonal and surgical revision, 'so that they can slip quietly into society as "normal" heterosexual males or females' (p. 21). These techniques of gender reassignment are legitimated through 'the assumption that in a sex-divided culture people can realize their greatest potential for happiness and productivity only if they are sure they belong to one of only two acknowledged sexes' (p. 21). It is noteworthy that the 'two-sexed world' was not always so: it is an historically specific reality, as Thomas Laqueur has observed (Laqueur, 1990).

Thus the reality of sexual dichotomy does not exist as a given but is achieved, and on a daily basis through various forms of practice. Our sense that there are men and women in the world is achieved through legal practices, through customs and attitudes and through various practices of alignment and correction which (through the physical force of the surgeon's knife or the chemical reactions associated with ingesting hormones) create a 'fit' between instances and categories, between the image of a two-sexed world and the otherwise 'reality' of anatomical diversity. (It is worth observing that intra-categorical differences between 'types of vaginas' are increasingly being asserted through media such as pornography, and through aesthetic and normative imageries promoted through cultures and procedures of cosmetic surgery. In the UK, according to a *Guardian* article there were 1118 labiaplasty operations performed by the NHS in 2008, in great part a response to the 'trickle up' porn-aesthetic in which female genitalia are both hairless and labia trimmed so as to seem 'pert' or excised completely [Myung-Ok Lee, 2011]. Nature, in other words, is tailored so as to look 'more natural'.) As Fausto-Sterling observes, diversity could be celebrated rather than erased, feared or ridiculed, but such a vision would depend upon the shifting assumptions about how anatomical and sexual 'reality' (realities) might look.

Fausto-Sterling's comments on, as it were, heterogeneous biological reality takes us to the first key lesson of slow sociology; namely, that reality is often more complex, more malleable and more uncertain than our otherwise 'hard and fast' notions of reality imply. This complexity is often simplified, streamlined and even caricatured, and in ways that in turn create trouble for actual instances of reality. In the case of biological sex, the division between men and woman is a *false dichotomy*, 'an illusion … that the disjunctive premise [one is either a man or a woman] presents jointly exhaustive alternatives' (Hurley, 2008: 154). Thus, following Hurley, to say 'either Mary is a woman or she *must* be a man' (note the word 'must' again) is to suggest a misplaced necessity: Mary *has to* belong to one or the other category, just as one might say, 'Mary must have a new car or she will become very sad': in either case, we can say that these conclusions are not necessarily true. Mary might manage to avoid unhappiness ('Get a grip Mary! Think about more important things! It's only a stupid car!') and Mary might, in a different classification system, be able to be something other than male or female. This is very different from saying that Mary is either at Max's house or she is walking in the park. In the latter statement, there is a necessity that one of these is false if the other is true ('As far as I know, people can't be in two places at once').

When I alluded, in the Introduction to this book, to the question of how opportunities and possibilities for action are distributed by the ways that realities are assembled, I was also implicitly addressing the ways in which false dichotomies (such as the male/female dichotomy) can lead to a 'slippery slope' of (unintended) consequences. Those consequences include what men and women can do, what they are expected to do, and how the categories of being known as 'male or female' are lodged within complex institutional arrangements and legal practices. Social, technological and cultural practices, in other words, iron out the manifold, crumpled textures of things, by formulating them in terms of over-arching, general categories of things within the world. And while it would be absurd to deny family resemblances between things it is nonetheless important to understand perceived similarity in relation to search criteria, to *decisions*, whether explicit or implicit, about what constitutes 'sameness'.

THE ARGUMENT OF THE BEARD

These points can be clarified through reference to a fallacy in informal logic known as the argument of the beard. As Walton puts it, drawing upon a 1930 article by Thouless, the reality of a beard can be called into question by asking how many hairs on the chin are required for the beard to be a beard. Is it one? Two? Is it 30? At some stage we will say, 'now that's a beard, not just a few straggly facial hairs.' Then, at that point, an opponent might counter, 'Why is thirty hairs a beard but not twenty nine? Or why twenty nine hairs but not twenty?' On this matter, Walton quotes another philosopher, Thouless (Walton, 1996: 237):

> ... by this process of adding one hair at a time, we can reach a number of hairs which would undoubtedly make up a beard. The trouble lies in the fact that the difference between a beard and no beard is like the difference between white and grey in the fact that one can pass by continuous steps from one to the other.

Walton then continues:

> The argument of the beard, so described, rests on the premise of a sequence of what Thouless calls 'continuous variation' – a continuum along which there is no precise cutoff point so that you can say, exactly at this point, one thing changes to another distinctly different thing. For example, there is no numerically exact point say, the difference between twenty-nine and thirty hairs – that is the difference between having a beard and not having a beard. Or in a continuum of shading from black to white, there is no single point where you can say, 'Here is the exact point of difference between white and grey.' Of course, you could arbitrarily define or stipulate such a point. But then, as Thouless astutely points out, a critic could 'pour scorn' on the arbitrariness of that proposal. (Walton, 1996: 237)

So is there then 'no difference' between having or not having a beard? Or, to return to the example from Fausto-Sterling, no difference between people who are male and people who are female? Surely, one might counter, 'it must be' that such a position is absurd? The point is that there are other, perhaps equally persuasive, ways to draw lines between categories because, as Walton observes, line drawing is done for human convenience. It is linked, in other words, to the perpetuation of certain forms of life. This notion of categorical difference as offering 'convenience' is akin to the idea that humans are often 'cognitive misers' (Fiske and Taylor, 1984), engaging in the minimal of cognitive effort rather than fully engaging with each and every occasion and set of stimuli encountered on an individual basis. Categories suffice because they have at least a modicum of similarity to reality; for example, a beard does consist of hairs on the face, though how many hairs make a beard is subject to debate. Taking a cue from Fausto-Sterling on the possibility of five sexes as discussed earlier, there could be a 'five-bearded' typology versus beard or no-beard, or there could be a false beard, pasted on. Thus, the instances of what we take to be forms of reality will not be identical to our conventional categories of reality (some beards will be sparse; some non-beards will be called beards if, for example, they appear on women or young boys who try to 'grow a beard'!). The sense of reality of a thing is, in other words, *enacted* by materials, technologies and practices of line drawing, and among these are our ways of talking about (comparing and classifying) those things which assert notions of how the lines between similarity and difference come to be drawn. Walton concludes:

> All natural language criteria for classifying individuals based on a verbal criterion tend to be inherently vague. But such a criterion can be made precise (or more precise, i.e. less vague). But either way, an opponent can attack the argument. She can say, 'That criterion is vague, therefore it is no good to make the sufficiently precise criterion needed in this case.' As a response the proponent can make the criterion more precise, say, by quantifying it in a numerical way. But then the opponent can attack the new version of the criterion as arbitrary, by citing a borderline case where no non-arbitrary basis for the inclusion (or exclusion) of a specific case is feasible. (1996: 257)

Returning from the relatively simple form of classification (beard, no-beard) to the more complex example from Fausto-Sterling (male/female), reality is neither 'in' nature, pre-existing human creative activity, nor is it fully a cultural construction (the reality of the beard is linked to the actuality of hair on the face, which is abstracted as the category, 'beard'). But Fausto-Sterling also compellingly highlights just how unruly nature can be, how it defies simple cultural classifications that, literally, in this case have to cut parts of it away if they are to seem realistic. If these points were not clear enough already, they are further clarified through the next example where it is possible to follow the biological sex of one person as it takes its definition (and changes) in relation to the technologies used to assess it.

CASE STUDY   The Olympic Committee on who is and is not male

Fausto-Sterling shows us how the complexity of sexual status is effaced through medical technologies in ways that both produce and reinforce the notion of a two-sexed world. Her work focused on a set of conventions for line drawing: the observation and classification of genitalia, their supposed bifurcation in nature and their subsequent clarification in culture. In short, the reality of biological sexual identity takes shape in relation to, and is enacted through, human-made tests and techniques. Depending upon which techniques are employed, the sexual status of individual bodies may be altered.

Consider sexual verification in sport. Prior to 1968, sexual verification at the Olympics consisted of a naked line-up combined with gynaecological exams. No vagina, no uterus, no eligibility. After 1968 it consisted of a smear that allowed chromosomes to be examined under a microscope: even if the athlete possessed a vagina, now only a double X chromosome would allow 'her' to be eligible to compete as a woman. Circa 2012, the criteria shifted again to tests for hyperandrogenism, levels of testosterone in the blood that are equivalent to 'male-level'. Such 'female' athletes are deemed ineligible to compete though they can regain eligibility if they medically reduce their testosterone levels. Thus, the reality of biological sexual identity shifts according to its technologies of verification; if measured one way, a person counts as female, if measured in another, as male. The question for these athletes then is which test offers the 'official' pronouncement on sexual identity. And yet, as Andre Banks, Director of LGBT protest group All Out.org, aptly put it, '[b]iology and humans are much more diverse than we would ever guess – what makes someone a man or a woman can't be identified in a single test or using a single measurement' (Reid Smith, 2012; see also All Out, 2012).

We have so far been considering how things that are different come to be understood as, or given the sense of being, things that are 'really' the same. And we have so far considered examples relating to sex/gender. We need also to consider examples of things that are seemingly identical but which, when examined closely, might seem unique. Taking a break from sex/gender examples, and considering something that might seem unproblematic – the case of 'identical' mass-produced objects – consider the case of Coca-Cola bottles. According to musician and philosopher John Cage:

> If I look at a Coca-Cola bottle and then look at another Coca-Cola bottle I want to forget the first one, in order to see the second coca-cola bottle as being original. And it is original, because it's in a different position in space and time and light is shining on it differently, so that no two coca-cola bottles are the same. (Cage, 2009)

As Cage suggests, coke bottles vary *in relation to* qualities of light (sunlight, northlight, evening light, candlelight, floodlight, fluorescent light), differences in position in space and time (indoors, outdoors, on a formal dinner table, in a petrol station soda machine), through their pairing with other things (a crystal decanter that highlights its more rough hewn appearance, a hand that is holding it as a weapon), and through the interpretive and experiential orientations that we bring to the scene, some of which may in turn be mediated by advertising or biographical memory (coke at holiday time, 'I'd like to teach the world to sing', and so on). All of these things can render a seemingly identical object in many different ways, some of which may seem to contradict each other (e.g., how can the bottle be both beautiful and ugly, green and white, small and large, opaque and translucent?). How this interplay takes shape, and with what consequences and under what circumstances, are questions that lie at the heart of any project concerned with interpreting – and changing – the world. How, then, are realities made real and real in their consequences? As we shall see, that is a question about the relationship between culture, materials, action and perception.

PART 2

CULTURAL SOCIOLOGY

3

CULTURALLY FIGURED REALITY

One of the best-known aphorisms in sociology is the so-called Thomas Theorem:

> When men [*sic*] define situations as real they are real in their consequences. (Thomas and Thomas, 1928: 51–2)

The idea is that social realities (situations) gain status *as* realities when people believe in them and thus act toward them *as if* they are real. Sometimes this theorem is compared to the Heisenberg Uncertainty Principle, the notion that physical matter behaves differently when it is being observed. (The popular understanding of the uncertainty principle is that particles are 'disturbed' by the attempt to measure them – as if they exist but can't be quantified. There is a more sophisticated interpretation that says what matters here is the *relationship* between measurement and measured.) So the Thomas Theorem can be understood as a way of describing how attitudes, characterisations and behaviours toward things are constitutive of the reality of things. Anyone who has ever found themselves in a situation where they were subject to some form of – as they saw it – unfair evaluative identification (deemed guilty, unintelligent, dull, a bad cook, ugly, a bad dancer, ill) and yet unable to shift the terms will understand the Thomas Theorem from, perhaps bitter, experience. Here, then, is one of the core 'problems' of sociology: how people are aligned with categories of identity and how that alignment has consequences – entitlements to action and action opportunities for example – and thus also politics. A famous study by David Rosenhan illustrates just how significant those consequences can be.

CASE STUDY   Rosenhan on 'Being Sane in Insane Places'

Writing at a time (1973) when psychiatry in the USA was undergoing critical re-evaluation and when a wave of scholars within psychiatry,

(Continued)

psychology and sociology were questioning the validity of psychiatric diagnoses – most notably, Erving Goffman, R.D. Laing, Theodore Sarbin, Thomas Scheff, and Thomas Szasz (see Pickering, 2010: 171–214) – Stanford professor David Rosenhan conducted a notorious experiment in social classification. He asked, simply, how can we tell the difference between the normal and abnormal, the sane and the insane? The problem, he suggested, is fraught. Rosenhan acknowledged that some behaviours (e.g., murder) are universally viewed as deviant (though what counts as murder, and what by contrast as legitimate violence ['casualties of war'] is often the subject of controversy). He also acknowledged that there can be severe forms of personal anguish that we may come to call 'mental illness'; he nonetheless suggested that '[w]hat is viewed as normal in one culture may be seen as quite aberrant in another ... [n]ormality and abnormality, sanity and insanity, and the diagnoses that flow from them may be less substantive than many believe them to be' (pp. 250–1). Thus, for Rosenhan an important question for social research is, 'do the salient characteristics that lead to diagnoses reside in the patients themselves or in the environments and contexts in which observers find them?' (p. 251).

Rosenhan suggested, as he put it, that '[g]ains can be made in deciding which of these perspectives is more nearly accurate by getting normal people (that is, people who do not have, and have never suffered, symptoms of serious psychiatric disorders) admitted to psychiatric hospitals and then determining whether they were discovered to be sane, and if so, how' (p. 251). Rosenhan reasoned that if the 'sanity' of such pseudo-patients was detected then there might be a case in favour of the idea that a sane individual 'can be distinguished from an insane context in which he is found'. On the contrary, if the sanity of the pseudo-patients was never discovered, then the traditional modes of psychiatric diagnosis could be called into question.

Rosenhan then arranged for eight 'sane' people (one graduate student, three psychologists, one paediatrician, one psychiatrist, a painter and a housewife – of this group three were women) to gain covert admission to 12 different hospitals (in five different states on the East and West coasts) under circumstances where only the hospital administrator and chief psychologist knew the 'true' identity of the pseudo-patients. On arrival, each pseudo-patient complained that she or he had 'been hearing voices' which were unclear but which spoke the words 'empty', 'hollow' and 'thud'. Beyond this initial statement of symptoms, the pseudo-patients gave actual life history data and after being admitted they ceased to simulate any symptoms of abnormality and to behave 'normally' from then on, explaining when asked that they no longer experienced any symptoms.

The pseudo-patients were uniformly admitted to hospital and each was required by the experiment to get out of hospital by convincing staff that he or she was sane. The length of hospitalisation of these pseudo-patients ranged from seven to 52 days, with an average of 19 days.

In a follow-on experiment, staff in a research and teaching hospital were informed that at some time during the next three months, one or more pseudo-patients would attempt to gain admission. Each member of staff was then asked to rate each patient at admission according to the likelihood that the patient was a pseudo-patient, using a 10-point scale. Of the 193 patients judged in this way, 41 were alleged – with a high degree of confidence – to be pseudo-patients by at least one member of staff; 23 were considered to be possible pseudo-patients by at least one psychiatrist; and 19 were suspected by at least one psychiatrist and one other staff member. In fact, no genuine pseudo-patient from Rosenhan's group actually presented themselves in the three-month period. Rosenhan concluded that 'any diagnostic process that lends itself so readily to massive errors of this sort cannot be a very reliable one' (p. 179).

As we can see from Rosenhan's study, judgement and interpretation are, in other words, causal factors in the process of reality creation. This idea points to other associated matters such as the concept of self-fulfilling prophecy (I believe that I will fail and then I do), the Matthew effect (we believe that someone is talented and we give them the things that nurture their talent and our perception of that talent), and even the placebo effect (we believe we have been given a medicine that will make us better and we do indeed feel better even when the medicine is nothing more than a sugar pill). Thus, the Thomas Theorem – its usefulness but also its limits – offers an excellent *point of departure, but not a terminus*, for our consideration of realities in everyday life.

The Thomas Theorem has fascinated generations of students. It is often interpreted as saying something like: 'Things are only real because we say, and believe, they are real: belief is powerful, reality outside of belief (or assertion) is weak'. This interpretation is simplistic; it offers at once too little and too much. How, for example, are realities named? What is the social structure of that process? For example, which definitions are voiced but go unheard? How, moreover, is the naming of situations linked to culturally and historically specific discourses or ways of naming, to categories, classification systems and modes of expression? And finally, how is there more to it than mere talk? How is situation definition linked to material settings, to the built environment, and indeed to situations that require actors to define situations?

The Rosenhan study is useful for developing and clarifying what all this might mean. First, Rosenhan is clear that our sense of the reality that someone is suffering from schizophrenia is not the result of one person or a group of people simply saying that this is so. This misses the question of where labels come from and why they take the forms and associated actions that they do. At issue here is the question of how labels come to be applied within physically or symbolically bounded settings characterised by hierarchies, understandings and organisationally patterned practices. These settings can be understood to be characterised by cultural meaning systems insofar as they are places where certain identities and forms of action prevail and are believed in, and where there are notions about how and where these forms can and should be recognised and addressed. So, within the institutional reality of the mental hospital, certain incorrigible assumptions prevail; for example, if someone shows 'classic' signs of being mentally unwell, they are treated as if they are mentally unwell to the extent that the identity of being unwell comes to anchor further observations and interpretations of their behaviour. In this process, the pseudo-patient's identity is transfigured: it is resituated against the ground of institutional assumptions and practices, lodged within a new system of meaning and action, in other words. This transfiguration will be a critical component of all that follows in the arguments I make below. Here, what is important is the 'Catch-22' that this transfiguration involves: all of the pseudo-patient's subsequent behaviour will be read as if it further elaborates the initial (and increasingly incorrigible) proposition of their diagnosed identity. So how does this happen?

To lay the groundwork for an answer to that question, I turn to two figures from classical sociological theory, Karl Marx (whom we met briefly in the Introduction) and Emile Durkheim, generally hailed as the father of current-day cultural sociology. I will describe and contrast their views on culture so as to highlight two key themes that will undergird everything that follows: first, the importance of material praxis and, second, the importance of culturally coded realities. There are politics involved in these transfigurations: by which assessments, which tests and measures, which technologies, is someone deemed 'insane'? (As opposed to, say, 'difficult to live with' or 'eccentric' or 'peculiar' or even just 'different'.) Realities, in other words, take shape through things beyond mere assertion, through material practice and through technological mediators.

MATERIALIST CONCEPTIONS OF WHERE REALITIES COME FROM

As the examples of sex/gender difference, discussed in Chapter 2, made clear, understanding realities as the products of human practice is not, in other words, the same thing as saying that reality can be whatever we say it is, or whatever we think it is. The examples of sex assignment in particular highlighted how categories that we take to be 'real' are mediated and made manifest through objects, tools and material practices. Situations are defined, in other words, by more than words. They are defined – realised – through material instruments, through forms of measurement and through the ways that humans and objects come to be linked.

This focus on material practice offers the best possible counter to the idea that realities are all in our minds (idealism), mental constructs, disconnected to the material world, and therefore merely assertions. Such a position omits the matter of what we do in concert with other people and what we do with things to make realities apparent. And to speak of what we do with things raises questions about the opposite question, namely, what things do with *us*. The question is what kinds of things, including interpretations and representations of things, do things do with us?

Doing things with things is an important starting point for what follows, and it will recur throughout as an undergirding theme, to be developed explicitly in Chapters 6 and 7. For now, it helps to introduce the first of the most important concept pairings for the argument to be presented in this book – materialism and the importance of social practice. Karl Marx's oft-quoted sentences from the 1852 essay on complex political struggle, 'The Eighteenth Brumaire of Louis Bonaparte', encapsulates the ways in which realities are made in specific circumstances, how they are not preordained but produced in relation to perceived social relations, situations, settings, conventions and prior practices, and with materials, media and tools that pre-exist any one actor. People, Marx says, make their own history *but*:

> they do not make it as they please; they do not make it under self-selected circumstances, but under circumstances existing already, given and transmitted from the past. The tradition of all dead generations weighs like a nightmare on the brains of the living. And just as they seem to be occupied with revolutionizing themselves and things, creating something that did not exist before, precisely in such epochs of revolutionary crisis they anxiously conjure up the spirits of the past to their service, borrowing from them names, battle slogans, and costumes in order to present this new scene in world history in time-honored disguise and borrowed language. (1972 [1852]: 245)

Marx reminds us that change can occur but not in wholly unconstrained ways and not through the assertion of mere will. To the contrary, when

I make or seek to change existing conditions I must act in specific milieux. And this situation within specific worlds means that I need to use tools, techniques and building blocks that are part of those worlds. And those things will affect what I can do, say and imagine. I act, in other words, using media and objects that were made by others.

To take a simple example, if I seek to build a house I will need to use building materials that are available to me and in relation to the kind of climate that pre-exists my desire for shelter. If those materials are bricks, wood, stone or mud the house will of necessity vary and the tools and skills involved will vary. These variations will constrain the kind of house I am able to build. So too, if the area I wish to build in is prone to heavy winds, rain or flooding, again, my house will need to take a particular form if it is to endure. I may have the desire to innovate but that desire is mediated and tempered by what can be done (or rather what I can do) with the materials at hand, the conventions available, the tools of the trade and how I learn to use these tools.

So too with technologies that assess difference – between types of people or between other sorts of phenomena. Consider how the pseudo-patients described above could not be recognised as 'insane' if they were not subject to pre-given, institutionally located diagnostic tests by which their mental status came to be registered (and came to 'stick'). Materials 'enable and constrain' us, in other words; they can serve to highlight differences and divisions, and they can also suppress even the perception of those differences.

Thus, as Marx observes, we may seek to instigate dramatic change – in any number of realms, for example, politics, economics, the arts, religion. To do so, however, and to galvanise supporters, we may mount a campaign that borrows language and imagery from the past, so as to dramatise our cause. As we do, our cause is deflected, mediated; it takes some of its identity from those images and that language in ways that, simultaneously, reinvent tradition and traditionalise invention. So we steer a course between what we might 'will' and what we are able to achieve. That course is steered through culture, both material and symbolic. Thus culture – understood in the Marxian sense as a building block of change and, more broadly, of social praxis – is causal, or rather it is a mediating factor, a dynamic ingredient in the making of reality. For Marx, however, culture is *a tool* that, as he describes it, is put into the 'service' of change, of social improvement. There is, in other words, an instrumentalist slant to the Marxian conception of culture.

Marx was not ultimately concerned with the question of how culture influences action, and thus with an explicitly cultural understanding and explanation of the sources and structures of action. And yet if, as Marx suggested, culture (material and symbolic) is a medium for action (resources for acting), then the study of what it means to say that culture is a medium for action, or, more bluntly, how culture works, is of paramount importance for all of sociology. This point can be illustrated yet more clearly by turning to a second classic sociological figure, Emile Durkheim.

DURKHEIM ON CULTURE AS THE REALM OF THE REAL

To introduce Durkheim, it is worth returning to Marx's point about 'borrowed language'. Durkheim also discusses this theme. In an important passage from *The Rules of Sociological Method*, Durkheim describes what he means by the term 'social fact', a social circumstantial feature that stands outside of individuals and which imparts structure to individuals' acts. To illustrate the concept, he too speaks of the inevitability of linguistic convention:

> When I perform my duties as a brother, a husband or a citizen and carry out the commitments I have entered into, I fulfill obligations which are defined in law and custom and which are external to myself and my actions. Even when they conform to my own sentiments and when I feel their reality within me, that reality does not cease to be objective, for it is not I who have prescribed these duties; I have received them through education ... Not only are these types of behavior and thinking external to the individual but they are endued with a compelling and coercive power by virtue of which, whether he wishes it or not, they impose themselves upon him ... I am not forced to speak French with my compatriots, nor to use the legal currency, but it is impossible for me to do otherwise. If I tried to escape the necessity, my attempt would fail miserably. (Durkheim, 1982 [1895]: 50–1)

Here we see, as with Marx, the ways in which our acts are played out under circumstances that are not of our own choosing. It is important to note that Durkheim does not describe culture as 'forcing' people to act within its parameters but rather that action will be un-action-able or ineffectual if it does not proceed from within socially shared and socially recognisable structures. If I abandon French, for example, in favour of a private 'language' known only to me, I will have, as the critical psychiatrist Thomas Szasz put it, 'a problem in living' (Szasz, 1960: 113). In other words, my society may deem me 'mad'. This is because, above all else, culture is the medium within which action, motive, ambition, desire, consciousness of the world and experience can be shared, exchanged and validated. This need to coordinate with others is what makes social facts into 'facts', or rather, into aspects of the world with which individuals must reckon.

Thus, as members of collectivities we attempt to frame our acts in relation to categories that will be recognisable by, and accountable to, others. To speak, we use (and are taught) conventions, materials and languages that pre-exist and exist between us, that broker the world. In our day-to-day existence we enter into and mould action around roles, identities and institutional relationships. Even our most private and personal emotional experience takes shape in relation to cultural media – in music, novels and art, for example, we learn about the shapes, imageries, intensities and temporalities of feeling forms which to greater and lesser extents can be understood to afford emotional, subjective experience.

Durkheim's vision highlights culture as it draws individuals out from the realm of private experience and effectively lifts them on to social terrain. It is in relation to these things that experience takes recognisable shape, that it is resolved into something that can be 'known'. Culture – aesthetic media, forms of language, currency, conventions, custom – gives form to experience and, indeed, to our otherwise amorphous will and desires. Writes Simon Frith, quoting George Elliot, '"Hetty had never read a novel . . . how then could she find a shape for her expectations?" Popular culture has always meant putting together a people rather than simply reflecting or expressing them' (Frith, 1990: 363).

Thus, while Marx's notion of culture was tinged with utilitarianism, in Durkheim (and even in this relatively early phase of Durkheim's work – *The Rules* was published nearly 20 years before his more extensive study of culture, *The Elementary Forms*), culture stands *before* action as a refracting device, mediator or filter and (as we began to explore through the example of biological sex) constitutive ingredient of what we come to know as 'nature'. So, too, agency (our ability to act in and on the world, to coordinate with others) is formulated through and in relation to the symbolic categories, sequences and images that culture provides. So, to use Durkheim's example (quoted above), if I am forced to speak French, I may find myself uttering idiomatic phrases, making use of communicative styles and even feeling sentiments and emotions that, were I to speak in English or German, might have been absent (cf. stereotypes such as 'Italian is the language of music, French the language of love ...'). Indeed, I might find that within any language what I set out to say, and what I began with, comes to be transformed or, a better term, traduced (changed in ways that betray the earlier sense): the linguistic materials constrain and enable the ways I can be expressive, and, therefore, who I am and what I can do. Work in translation studies, and observations from people who are multilingual, highlight how there are some things that are simply easier to say in one language rather than another.

The same is true of discourses, or stylistically and poetically patterned ways of speaking within a language. We speak, for example, of 'discourses of romantic love' and 'discourses of individualism'. And scholars have examined how certain forms of thought or action can be impeded when discourses become deep-seated within a group's patterned ways of communicating; for example, the authors of *Habits of the Heart* described how Americans find it difficult to speak of commitment and community because of highly prevalent and prominent discourses of self-actualisation and individual fulfilment (Bellah et al., 1985). Such discourses make it difficult to articulate some of the tacit and more communal practices that are part of American lives but which are hidden from 'view' because they are wordless.

Nowhere is Durkheim's theory of culture's constitutive role stated more clearly than in his famous essay, *The Elementary Forms of Religious Life*. There, Durkheim shows us how the 'modern' and 'primitive' [sic] minds are alike. All classificatory systems, Durkheim argues, derive from collective life. There is no divide between 'scientific' and 'rational' societies and those who believe in magic, totems and gods. To the contrary, in all societies, what passes as reality, Durkheim says, *emerges* from collective systems of belief that imbue the world with symbolic character. The soldier, for example, who conflates the flag of his/her country with the country itself is experiencing a 'reality' through emblems, totems and images. Putting this slightly differently, Durkheim argues, we apprehend 'reality' through symbolic mediators, or 'forms' of societal belief systems (of which religion is one). These mediators become, as it were, sacred (items of faith) and their sacred status (their reality) is conserved through collective patterns of ritual enactment associated with these realities, and with strictures governing the ways these realities can be approached.

For Durkheim, then, culture is not merely ideological, and is much more than a means to an end, no matter how much we might emphasise the ways in which the means may mediate the achievement of the end. On the contrary, and much more 'strongly', culture constitutes the terms and temper of social interaction and thus reality creation. In particular, Durkheim points us to the matter of consciousness, collectively formed and formulating individual orientation, perception, action and will. The anthropologist Mary Douglas put this point succinctly in her famous work *Purity and Danger* (to which we will return). She said:

> Culture, in the sense of the public, standardised values of a community, mediates the experience of individuals. It provides in advance some basic categories, a positive pattern in which ideas and values are tidily ordered. (Douglas, 2002 [1966]: 40)

The world of ideas and belief is, in other words, a world *sui generis*, a world in its own right, not one reducible to other factors. Indeed, it *is* the world within which action and experience takes place and the world from within which one may take comfort from the possibility of shared and sharing, knowing and communicating, experience. It is, moreover, distressful when the possibility for this sharing is not available.

> ## CASE STUDY   Richard Hilbert on pain and anomie
>
> If I feel pain, or even a vague form of malaise – lethargy, weakness, unfocused anxiety – I need to communicate what that feels like and to do that I need to use modes of expression that are outside of my sensations. So you might ask me, on a scale of 0 to 10 how bad is the pain? At that moment I am being asked to, and attempting to, translate an individual experience into something socially knowable, something outside both me and you. In making that translation, however, I may also modify the original sensations. I say, 'I think it's about a 5'. And you then say, 'Well that is reassuring, since last week you thought it was an 8.' I might then re-experience my condition in relation to this new depiction. As such, something outside of me has given shape and definition to something inside. If, on the other hand, I am unable to describe my sensation, to give it socially sharable form, I am left in a kind of incommunicable limbo which brings with it additional forms of distress because it isolates me. I cannot get anyone to understand my pain.
>
> Richard Hilbert has examined this issue in relation to the condition of chronic back pain. As Hilbert describes that condition, it is often intractable both to cure and to explanatory diagnosis. When the cause of the pain cannot be identified, Hilbert explains, pain sufferers experience a form of anomic distress, a sense of uncertainty or, more forcefully, 'a withdrawal of reality and the possibility of objective experience' (Hilbert, 1986: 1) in which pain is experienced in a-cultural terms. The fact that the source, nature and form of pain remains unidentified creates, Hilbert says, a form of uncertainty, and thus the pain, while felt and experienced, is indescribable and thus sets the sufferer outside of the kinds of social circles where the 'reality' of the pain can be discussed and shared, and this alienation becomes yet another source of suffering.

The social is, in other words, not identical with reality – though it is informed by reality – but it is the *realm* or, as I shall describe in Chapters 5 and 7, the realms, within which we are able to achieve a sense of reality. Thus, according to Durkheim, and as illustrated through Hilbert's study of chronic but unexplainable pain, it is not possible to stand apart from culture (objectivity, neutrality) in the way that we stand apart from, for example, a physical toolkit (I am here, it is there), because it is only through culture that reality can emerge *as* reality. Linked to this understanding, and also Durkheimian, there are no aims, ambitions or interests that are not formulated in relation to cultural frameworks and their associated systems of belief ('religion is above all a system of notions by which individuals imagine the society to which they belong' [Durkheim, 2001 (1912): 170–1]). So, for example, if I feel the desire for wealth (I wish I had a trillion dollars) or status (I wish I were the US President) these desires have been articulated through cultural categories and cultural models which offer both ends and means for action. In Durkheim's account, we are always inside culture and it is from within cultural frameworks that action, orientation, feeling and aspiration take shape.

Culture is, in other words, the medium of our collective existence; it facilitates coordination and mutual attunement:

> Social life, then, in every aspect and throughout its history, is possible only thanks to a vast body of symbolism. The material emblems, the embodied representations with which we are especially concerned in the present study, are a particular form of that symbolism. But there are many others. Collective feelings can be embodied equally in personalities or formulas: some formulas are flags; some personalities, real or mythic, are symbols … (Durkheim, 2001 [1912]: 177)

We are drawn into and come to inhabit and enact realities through their representation in 'formulas', Durkheim says. Realities, then, according to Durkheim, are not brute facts but are rather formulated, produced through cultural arrangements and shared conventions. This drawing-into-formulation is accomplished through ritual processes, coordinated and reiterated, patterned practices, along with social and physical rhythm. It is thus through cultural imagery and cultural praxis that we become human social beings, that we are, as it were, *lifted* into a shared world. Without the benefit of that elevation, or virtual enhancement, we are bereft of culture – in Hilbert's and Durkheim's terms, anomic. Culture, in other words, lies at the heart of *all* sociological forms of enquiry. To examine this claim we will now explore what is sometimes called the 'strong programme' of cultural sociology, a programme in which reality is emphatically understood as always culturally formulated.

THE 'STRONG PROGRAMME' OF CULTURAL SOCIOLOGY

Durkheim is frequently hailed as the first fully fledged *cultural* sociologist (Alexander and Smith, 1988, 2001) and his work has inspired a growing body of work within cultural sociology, cultural studies and post-struc-turalist theory. All three of these areas are concerned with, as Alexander puts it, how:

> rhetorics are cultural structures. They are deeply constraining but also enabling at the same time. The problem is that we don't understand them. This is the task of a cultural sociology. It is to bring the unconscious cultural structures that regulate society into the light of the mind … The secret to the compulsive power of social structures is that they have an inside. They are not only external to actors but internal to them. They are meaningful. These meanings are structured and socially produced, even if they are invisible. We must learn to make them visible … Cultural sociology is a kind of social psychoanalysis. Its goal is to bring the social unconscious up for view. To reveal to men and women the myths that think them so that they can make new myths in turn … (Alexander, 2003: 3–4)

As Alexander notes, social structures can be compulsive because they 'have an inside', they are meaningful articles of faith to those who believe in them. And so, culture can have serious consequences – as Rosenhan's study of admission to the mental hospital made clear (e.g., the doctors and hospital personnel had 'faith' in the reality of the pseudo-patients' illnesses). The next example, Isaac Reed's study of the Salem witch trials in colonial America, further illustrates the way in which cultural frameworks offer parameters for meaning and action, but also takes us further into the 'darker' side of what culture can do (and do to us).

CASE STUDY   Isaac Reed on 'Why Salem Made Sense'

In his study of the late 17th-century colonial Massachusetts, Isaac Reed asks the question, 'What drove the people of Salem to execute nineteen of their own men and women?' (Reed, 2007: 210). He suggests that it is all too easy to reduce the answer to this question to political, economic or social factors. To do so, however, misses an ethnographically sensitive focus on actors' motivations and subjectivi-ties and prevents the potentially inappropriate and often unacknowl-edged imposition of our own (researcher) values and orientations on subjects who acted in previous times. Instead, he suggests, we need to understand the 'texts' that were operant at the time and in the loca-tion of the action we seek to explain. These 'texts', he says, 'typified meanings which structure moments of faith and revelation, define the split between public denunciation and private skepticism, and also serve as a "model for" and "model of" social reality' (Reed, 2007: 210). In the case of Salem, Reed suggests, the witch trials made sense to participants because they were part of a cultural meaning system or 'set of actions in the defense of an emotionally charged order of morality, metaphysics, and sex' (p. 210). More specifically, the logic of what happened was driven by particular conceptions of gender and the ways in which 'troublesome' women meddled in the 'invisible world' outside the command of men. The crimes of the 'witches' were nothing less than these women's violations of the moral order. The real culprit was Puritan culture, which, as Reed suggests, possessed certain fault lines that created the reality of witchcraft. Being a witch was, in other words, a matter of positioning; its reality emerged relationally from within the patterned cultural fabric. Against the background of that pattern, gender transgression could be viewed as witchcraft, a figure in the foreground. Thus to be a witch was to be (perceived) in a culturally dangerous position in relation to the background cultural tapestry. To put this slightly differently, the meaning system that figured the concept of witchcraft highlighted important and increasingly salient tensions between magic and religion, and between the practical workings of the world and the condition of the individual soul (p. 229).

Reed takes this argument further in a book-length consideration of interpretation and theory in the social sciences. There, Reed suggests that the aim of interpretivism is:

> to grasp the meaningful world of Puritan life and, in particular, how witches and witchcraft played an emotionally charged role in the Puritan social imaginary, encoding a socially powerful metaphysics of God, sex, and patriarchy. What sort of knowledge claim is this interpretation? The point, with Salem at least, is that this metaphysics was threatened in 1692 by the possibility of witches meddling with the cosmos ... Who felt threatened by the witches? What did fear motivate those people to do, and what social processes were they able to trigger to get done what they were certain needed to be done? What were the unintended effects of these developments? These are causal, explanatory questions, and they force us to consider whether or not, and if so how, interpretations of social meaning can possess explanatory torque. (2011: 10–11)

Reed's argument pushes cultural sociology into the study of meaningful structures; how culture mediates realities through

(Continued)

(Continued)

the ways that it classifies and packages, through its patterns and through the ways - as with the case of the witches - that cultural patterns highlight or foreground anomalies. That which is deviant, dangerous or otherwise a threat is that which emerges as potentially contrary to the patterned background of the social fabric, something that stands out and clashes with its otherwise stable social life and its formal and cognitive arrangements. Reed thus highlights how culture is causal because meaningful forms affect action and perception - we 'see through' culture in two senses simultaneously: first, rather like a pair of spectacles on the nose of a regular eyeglass wearer, we become so familiar with cultural frames that we become unaware of their presence. Second, different cultural refractions enable and constrain us to 'see' in different ways (close up, but not far afield). Culture mediates our world while simultaneously offering us a mode of understanding that world. Those who felt threatened by the witches, in other words, were perceiving and acting within a cultural structure or matrix in which what the witches did 'really' threatened the fabric of Puritan society and thus 'really' had to be eradicated. So (as history has revealed repeatedly over the centuries) cultural prescriptions can be threatening; indeed they can be lethal. As Reed puts it, the problem of Salem was 'not a lack of reality but too much of it' (Reed, 2007: 230).

CULTURE, AND THE PROBLEM OF 'TOO MUCH REALITY'

The 'reality' that there were witches emerged from a cultural meaning system, one which, Reed argues, can explain historical events. Thus, Reed's perspective seeks to identify the ways in which realities emerge from, in Durkheim's words, a formula of the world. Within this purview of culture and its causal properties, events great and small can be understood in terms of the ways that social actors dwell within and take their cognitive cues from cultural forms. The shape that culture takes is consequential and thus it is vital that we, as scholars of social action, attend to cultural forms – to discourses, representations, texts, scripts, poetics and other forms of symbolic production.

As we have seen, social identities, emerging from cultural meaning systems, can be oppressive. In the Rosenhan study, the pseudo-patients' highly adhesive labels ('schizophrenic') came to be sticky, not because someone pronounced them 'ill', but because those pseudo-patients came to be fitted into a larger gestalt of what illness (versus wellness) looks like. From within those ways of seeing – Reed's 'too much' reality (Rosenhan speaks of this as 'contexts of stimuli around' individuals) – there was no compelling counter-script and no notion of mental health and illness as diverse and perhaps overlapping, rather than dichotomous, states of being. And so, as with the witches in Salem, the pseudo-patients came to be *held* in a particular interpretive slot or, as I will say later, framework, held within the hospital until further notice. Cultural sociology (understood, in Alexander's terms, as 'a kind of psychoanalysis') can illuminate the ways we come to 'act out', as it were, scenes and scenarios that circulate as part of the cultural repository of poetics, myth, legend, imagery and imagination (Alexander, 2003). This fundamentally Durkheimian concern with how culture gets into action is focused on how it is possible to see, *in action*, renditions and performances of cultural texts (think, for example, of how children imitate styles and roles associated with the adult world of action, playing dress-up or house – 'You be the baby and I'll be the mommy'). Through examination of cultural structures, Alexander and Reed suggest, we can uncover the deep rhetorical structures of the collective unconscious; we can understand why action took the courses and channels that it took.

So, for example, a 'strong' cultural sociology directs our attention to how individuals, organisations and parties 'hook their actions into the background culture ... working to create an impression of sincerity and authenticity rather than one of calculation and artificiality, to achieve verisimilitude' (Alexander and Mast, 2006: 1). Thus, one might seek to present oneself as a 'trustworthy' person, aligning oneself with the known insignia of trust – eye contact, demonstrative acts, a curriculum vitae of prior activities and testimonials from equally 'solid' referees. As such, one is engaging in what Erving Goffman (1959) spoke about as the presentation of self, the aligning of self with recognisable categories of identity (a type of person, an identity slot that exists in 'background' culture). To develop this point, and to move into the performative features of what it means to belong to a culture, let's return, once again, to the example of sex/gender difference. Only this time consider that topic from the point of view of how actors manage, in real time or 'local' situations, to 'pass' as fitting into one or the other of these categories (a topic we touched upon in Chapter 2). To consider this topic is to see how culture 'gets into' action, though there is much more to this story still to come. We are really only beginning to consider how culture is involved in the production of our senses of reality.

CASE STUDY   From Garfinkel to Butler: *performing* femininity

We have already debunked the idea that there are 'only' (or rather that there are 'clearly only') two distinct human biological sexes. Indeed, we have also considered how the concept of biological male-or female-ness is itself produced from within culture and through the technologies by which these concepts come to be registered, and the material and symbolic cultural practices that clarify them as distinct realities. It is now time to consider in more detail some of the ways in which we engage in practices (and not always with conscious reflection) that 'realise' the apparent given nature of our categories of the real. For this the work of two theorists, Harold Garfinkel and Judith Butler, is helpful.

In his 1967 collection of essays, *Studies in Ethnomethodology*, Harold Garfinkel wrote about the case of an 'intersexed' person known pseudonymously as Agnes. Agnes was (she recounted) born with an intersexed body (she possessed the primary sexual signs of a man but with secondary sexual traits of a female). At the time of Garfinkel's writing, Agnes was awaiting sex-reassignment surgery.

Garfinkel describes how Agnes engaged in what he termed passing practices, that is, how Agnes contrived to pass as a 'natural normal' female. In so doing he also documented some of the ways in which cultural categories are realised through social practices. So, for example, Agnes engaged in forms of action that were conducive to her construal as a 'natural normal' female: she chose to wear highly feminine forms of clothing (twin-set sweaters), she wish to pursued feminine hobbies and interests (cooking), and she avoided situations that might highlight her gender ambiguity (such as wearing a swimming costume at the beach – instead she remained clothed and announced that she had her period). In short, Agnes managed her self-presentation through a series of practices that foregrounded iconic aspects of feminine identity and suppressed counter-feminine (masculine) features. Garfinkel's description of Agnes' practices thus showed how gender is not a given, but is accomplished. It thus illuminated how one person could be seen to engage in the active documentation in the here and now of a more general cultural form, namely being a woman.

In Agnes' case, this production was overt, strategic. That was because Agnes' identity as a woman was in some respects problematic – her gender ambiguity was considerable. For other 'women', the production of femininity often occurs tacitly: one engages in depilation (see the earlier case study on body hair) and in the management of voice tone, dress and comportment without being fully conscious of what one is doing, following long-honed habits and practices that are, for all practical purposes, invisible. But the lessons from Garfinkel are more generally applicable; they illustrate how one comes to be known under the rubric of a categorical identity and they illuminate the frame-by-frame practices of passing as these are enacted by any would-be woman (or man).

While Garfinkel emphasised the practices by which one side of the sexual and gender dichotomy is realised in action, and where his handling of gender is seemingly a-political (but in fact trades, I would suggest, upon highly conventional assumptions about what femininity is), Judith Butler by contrast described how the categories to which Agnes was oriented, and which she sought to replicate – as a natural, normal woman – are themselves problematic, themselves performed, indeed, in and through reflexive attempts to achieve them. In *Gender Trouble: Feminism and the Subversion of Identity* (2006 [1990]), Butler showed how the category of women and womanliness is defined in ways that can be seen to be shaped by *institutionalised* forms of power and patriarchy. Deconstructing the 'illusion' of gender identity, Butler shows, like Garfinkel, how the apparent reality of gender is realised through scripts (images of gender as real) and performances.

In their respective treatments of passing practices and gender performances, and not withstanding the different theoretical resources and perspectives they employ, both Garfinkel and Butler offer more grist for the mill of the 'strong' cultural sociological approach. Both describe how cultural categories provide ends and containers for action (self-presentation, orientation, aspiration) and how actors reproduce these categories in and through social performance. We have come to a point where we can appreciate how cultural forms offer candidates and templates for action, how they offer structures against which actors can pattern themselves. But so far, this focus has been on, as it were, the outside of action, on how forms offer templates and exemplars against which action is modelled so as to present a verisimilitude of reality (in this case the reality of sex/gender identity). But to what extent is this performance more than staged? In what ways do the scripts and slots that culture provides structure the *inside* of action? How, in other words, does feeling, emotion and embodiment come to take on aspects of reality that provide 'real' forms of embodied, subjective experience? For if realities are to have a true sense of reality they also have to be felt.

4

ONCE MORE, WITH FEELING: BEYOND PERFORMANCE

While Garfinkel and Butler highlight how we perform ourselves categorically as types of being, and while Rosenhan's study highlights how we are often linked to categories against our personal preference or judgement, so far we have not considered the 'inside' of action. Our strongest senses of reality, in other words, are linked to emotions, feelings, sensations and other seemingly palpable forms of encountering the world. How is it then that, for all practical purposes, culture or general categories of being get under our skin and into corporeality? How does culture give shape and texture to subjectivity, to consciousness, and how, in adopting and seeking to reproduce certain forms (e.g., what women must look like, what the mentally healthy ought not to do), can we become *affected* by those forms?

We have already considered, via Hilbert's example of nameless back pain, how finding/being unable to find an 'objective' description of the phenomenon (and thus being drawn within, or being denied access to the symbolic fold of seemingly 'shared' or common knowledge/ experience) can affect our actual experience of pain (I will return to the example of pain in Chapter 8). So too, the impact of external structures can affect our psychodynamic states. For example, consider how, in attempting to 'put on a good front', perhaps to seem 'cheerful' for others, we may smile more than we actually feel like doing and cheer ourselves up in the process, walking with more of a spring in our step, lifting our head up a bit higher, feeling more energetic. This simple example highlights some of the ways in which social performance is by no means the same thing as mere play-acting or paying lip service to obligatory forms of reality. Far more powerfully, being deemed or feeling compelled to look or be 'like' something (one is deemed to be, say, ill, beautiful, a good cook, or one feels compelled to act like, say, a woman, professional, caring) can come to affect future action and orientation: we become that which we are hailed for being. In this way, 'situations defined as real' become 'real in their consequences'.

This process of becoming, which can look like what is sometimes termed self-fulfilling prophecy (you tell me that I will fail, I lose my nerve and, indeed, I fail), involves a form of circuitry. One becomes, and can come to internalise, the thing that one initially encountered as external. While there is an 'up side' to this circuitry (it is what enfolds us to human worlds), there is also a 'down side' as we began to explore through Rosenhan's study of being sane in insane places: we can find ourselves lodged into cultural spaces in ways that may make extricating ourselves difficult indeed (e.g., trying to 'kick' a habit or rehabilitate a reputation or challenge others' attitudes and assumptions about one's identity, ability, appearance or potential).

CASE STUDY   Getting into role: Hacking on looping

In *The Social Construction of What?* Ian Hacking (1999: Ch. 4) describes what he speaks of as two different 'kinds' of things – 'interactive' or 'human' kinds and 'indifferent' or 'natural' kinds. The former, Hacking maintains, are subject to a process to which he refers as 'looping effects'. Similar to the acoustical concept of a feedback loop (where some of the sonic output is fed back into the input in ways that permit adjustment and correction), the concept of looping refers to the process by which human behaviour, unlike forms of behaviour in the non-human, natural world, may be affected by the various ways in which humans come to be identified or classified. As Hacking puts it, 'people classified in a certain way tend to conform to or grow into the ways that they are described' (Hacking, 1995: 21). Classification, in other words, can affect self-experience.

So, for example, if an individual is diagnosed with a form of mental illness (Hacking uses the case of bi-polar syndrome) she or he may begin to act in ways that are aligned with what others – and increasingly she or he – expects to be typical given that diagnosis. She or he may say to themselves things such as, 'Well of course I cannot do this or that because of my bi-polar disorder'. As the individual's behaviour alters in relation to her/his classification, so too that person's behaviour loops back to affect the categories by which she or he came to be classified in the first place. And what is true for this individual, for this particular person 'with bi-polar', is also true of the collective of people 'with bi-polar': over time, the behaviours associated with being, for example, bi-polar can shift and thus reshape the boundaries of what it means to be bi-polar. There is, in short, an interaction between classification and behaviour over time, a looping effect.

Hacking understands mental illness as in part the artefact of cultural meaning systems, and as offering possibilities for action and experience within specific historical milieux. So, at different times in different places, some forms of behaviour are hailed as problematic and associated with pathological conditions. Just as one simply could not be hanged for being a witch in Salem circa 2014 but could in 1692, so too it was not possible to be identified as bi-polar in Salem of 1672 (as in the case study considered earlier by Reed), but entirely possible circa 2014. While this point may sound simplistic, it is not. It emphasises behavioural conditions (realities) as historically specific: one cannot contract a mental illness that one and one's culture do not already know and recognise – which is not to say that one might not exhibit behavioural symptoms and/or forms of distress.

Hacking's concept of looping highlights how we adopt cultural identifications, inserting ourselves into them and shaping ourselves in relation to them, and in ways that in turn modify those identifications iteratively. The concept is useful too for thinking about how it is we come to feel and embody particular stances and identities. That process involves a form of work or adjustment, what sociologist Arlie Hochschild terms 'emotional work', a 'bodily cooperation with an image, a thought, a memory – a cooperation of which the individual is aware' (Hochschild, 1979: 551). Hochschild's notion emphasises the often-tacit features of feelings' enculturation, how we may not be fully aware that we orient to images, thoughts or memories as templates for corporeal experience. This process is often socially structured as when we may seek to 'feel' in ways that we are encouraged, or required, to feel – as in workplace encounters where people may need to engage in activities that involve the selling of (emotion-laden) forms of service (flight attendants, but also waiters, sex workers, counsellors, hair dressers, funeral directors, and many others). At other times, our entry into what we assume are culturally prescribed and organisationally appropriate feeling forms may occur more habitually, or indeed under duress, as in the case of ascriptions of 'stigmatised' or subservient forms of identity. These forms may penetrate embodied experience, and indeed embodied response to external stimuli, as the next example illustrates.

CASE STUDY   Jackson and Scott on 'Faking Like a Woman'

Sexuality is sometimes thought to be linked to the 'natural', to for example the sex roles 'nature intended' for men and women. We have earlier considered how the male/female dichotomy is not 'natural' but rather natural/cultural (see 'Nobody's perfect' above) and thus it is possible to queer the notion that there are two sexes, biologically ordained (which is not to say that biology – in all of its complexity – does not play *any* role in determining social/sexual practices and conventions). So too, we should be critical of other attempts to essentialise male and female sexuality (that is, to argue that sexual preferences and associated forms of conduct are caused by natural biological differences). For example, as Jackson and Scott describe, sexuality is sometimes theorised – by psychoanalytically oriented feminists – as a property of the individual psyche, something that emanates from the unconscious and which is therefore mysterious.

In contrast to these views, Jackson and Scott locate sexuality in the context of social and sexual encounters and episodes. In so doing, they dismantle the black box of how sexual response unfolds within these actual encounters. More to the point, they examine the event of orgasm from the perspective of how embodied selves can be seen to be located in and displayed as interaction. As they put it, 'even this most individual, "private", "physical" experience is always also social' (Jackson and Scott, 2007: 96). At issue, then, as the authors describe, is how orgasm is practically accomplished, what it takes to produce its embodied and dramaturgical features. How then, they ask, do we acquire 'the cultural competencies that enable us to "know" what it is, to "recognize" it in ourselves and others' (p. 107).

Drawing upon Howard S. Becker's work on becoming a marijuana user (Becker, 1953), Jackson and Scott then go on to suggest a three-stage process: learning to engage, learning to perceive effects, and learning to define those effects as pleasurable. They also consider the provenance of learning resources, pointing to the media – movies, pornography and other places where one may locate what they term (drawing on Gagnon and Simon, 1974) 'sexual scripts' or narrative descriptions of what orgasm is and what it looks like. These are not fixed or deterministic but fluid, open: opportunities or pointers for improvisation. Of especial interest within Jackson and Scott's account is the issue of how the 'fake' and 'real' orgasm are both, as it were, culturally produced. As with Hochschild and her concept of emotional work, one learns to 'cooperate' with an image. They are realised, time and again, in open-ended but still structured ways. Thus, the authors conclude, 'just as a woman learns to "throw like a girl", so she later learns to fake [I will add here, experience] like a woman' (Jackson and Scott, 2007: 111).

So there is no preordained, natural way that the sexual should take shape or flow. And even the 'peak' experience of orgasm, Jackson and Scott argue, can be understood to take shape in relation to things outside of individuals. This focus on peak and, at least implicitly, on flow can be used to comment on some concepts current in social psychology, namely 'flow' (Csikszentmihalyi, 1990) and 'being in the zone'. The former, flow, is usually defined in relation to cognitive activities, as the ability to operate in and on the environment (including others) in ways that are effective, that are not ultimately blocked or thwarted. This flow sensation is a characteristic of enjoyment and absorption, or good fit with the environment(s) in which action occurs (a task at hand, a process, a situation – think interaction forms such as a conversation, or physical activity such as rowing a boat, experiencing orgasm, being part of a string quartet performance, knitting a blanket, riding a bicycle, or chopping an onion). It is the antithesis of anxiety on the one hand and boredom on the other (Csikszentmihalyi and Csikszentmihalyi, 1988) and it is linked to the ease with which one can accomplish a demanding task. 'Being in the zone' is more usually a term reserved for physical activities such as sport; it describes a sense of 'fit' between action and aspiration, a (sense of) synchronicity with the rhythm of things. Thus, and this is the most important feature of what Jackson and Scott have to say, cultural action is not only about *pretending* to be what we think or feel we 'ought' to be; such a vision of action overemphasises the strategic dimension of what we call agency. To the contrary, cultural action is also about how our emotional and indeed physical and physiological being takes shape in relation to culture. Hence one 'learns' how to experience the seemingly 'natural' event of sexual orgasm just as one 'learns', in varied ways (formally, informally), how to experience the seemingly merely physical effects of marijuana. In both cases, experience takes shape through iterated, conscious, unconscious, quasi-conscious, cultural (aesthetic, mimetic, practical) collaborative processes of physical, emotional and cognitive 'work' which in turn may be linked to forms of biofeedback – muscle memory, the development of blood vessels or strength, and other 'techniques of the body'. Following Mauss (1992: 455), these techniques highlight 'the ways in which, from society to society, men know how to use their bodies … it is essential to move from the concrete to the abstract and not the other way around'. This 'learning' is a form of 'work' – emotional, physiological, psychosocial, cultural. It is worth dwelling on what Mauss has to say on this topic.

Through a series of vivid, and often mundane examples (e.g., learning how to spit) Mauss describes how one embarks upon, often lifelong, apprenticeships to learn body techniques, at times having to learn things that seem to contradict instinctual habits (such as learning how to open the eyes under water when diving). He goes on to describe how the general activities that we assume are common to 'all' human beings instead can be understood to take shape in specific ways and thus may vary over time (he offers the example of changed styles of swimming) and place (the English Army does not march in the same way as the French, nor did it know, in the trenches of World War I, how to use a French spade [shovel] (Mauss, 1992: 456). As with learning how to 'fake' like a woman, so too one learns (and relearns) how to walk like a type of woman, as Mauss explains:

> I was ill in New York. I wondered where I had seen girls walking the way my nurses walked. I had the time to think about it. At last I realized that it was in movies. Returning to France, I noticed how common this gait was, especially in Paris; the girls were French and they too were walking in this way. In fact, American walking fashions had begun to arrive over here, thanks to the movies. This was an idea I could generalize. The positions of the arms and hands while walking form a social idiosyncrasy – they are not simply a product of some purely individual, almost completely psychic, arrangements and mechanisms … Finally … [i]n all these elements of the art of using the human body, the facts of education are dominant. The notion of education could be superimposed on that of imitation … prestigious imitation … The action is imposed from without, from above, even if it is an exclusively biological action involving his body … (Mauss, 1992: 457–9)

In recent years sociologists concerned with embodiment have explored how it is that individuals come to move in socially patterned ways, and how these movement styles are associated with durable embodied dispositions, ones that are often linked to social position (Bourdieu, 1984; Inglis, 2005). Often the term 'habitus' (originally from Mauss [1992] and subsequently developed by Bourdieu [1977]) is employed to capture the notion of unconscious but socially acquired dispositions, tastes and patterned embodied practices. So, in an autoethnography of how he became a boxer, Wacquant (2004) has described how this pugilistic disposition is fashioned through learning and apprenticeship, through repeated practice over time that takes shape through an embodied learning process. Similarly, Wainwright et al. (2006) have described the way ballet dancers learn, through repeated movements, time after time, how to become ballet dancers. More specifically, Wainwright et al. describe how the acquisition of embodied habitus can serve to highlight the similarities and differences between different types of habitus – an individual habitus (being a particular ballet dancer – Margot Fonteyn), a choreographic habitus (being able to embody a particular choreographer's vision) and an institutional habitus (being a member of a particular *corps de ballet*).

CASE STUDY   Embodying an ethos: *capoeira* with
Delamont and Stephens

In a nuanced, 'two-handed' ethnography (two researchers, one a participant, the other an observer) of *capoeira* classes (a Brazilian practice, part martial art, part dance) held in the UK, Delamont and Stephens (2008) develop the theory and ethnography of embodied acquisition. Drawing upon Atkinson's study of how an opera production comes to take on an overall grain or pattern and thus characteristic feel and style (Atkinson, 2006), Delamont and Stephens examine how the individual *capoeira* disposition takes shape over time through repeated movement and guiding talk (rhetoric). It is through iterative practice, and the judgement of the teacher-expert, that individuals come to pass on to higher gradations of *capoeira* expertise. In an associated publication (Delamont, 2006), Delamont describes how the 'expert body' is distinguished from the novice, or disciple, body. In both, the focus is on fine-grained learning over time, on becoming the phenomenon through repetitive practice understood as the means by which otherwise disparate physical actors come to coordinate and, to some extent, share embodied patterns, orientations and their associated feeling states. Culture does not automatically determine bodily practices but is rather learned through practice over time. Thus Delamont and Stephens' work highlights how, if we are to understand how culture gets into action, we need to engage in painstaking scrutiny of the actual processes that give rise to embodied forms of being and experiencing, because, as Delamont and Stephens observe, quoting Bourdieu (1977: 72), 'Capoeira is a paradigm case of an embodied social practice that is "collaboratively orchestrated" and "regular", without being "the product of obedience to rules" or "the orchestrating action of a conductor" ' (Delamont and Stephens, 2008: 70).

So far, I have sketched a vision of culture that is structuralist or, a term I prefer, formulating (following on from the discussion of Durkheim's formulae above), though increasingly, as the last set of examples on embodied dispositions illustrates, this structuralist perspective has involved a focus on the ways in which culture (models, templates, descriptions, images) 'get into' action. The term 'structuralist' is used because it implies a connection between surface-level forms of action (in the here and now, what we do) and 'underlying' or 'deeper' rules, codes and tacit understandings (how we typically do things).

To put this slightly differently, so far I have been describing a vision of interactionist and interpretive cultural sociology focused on the ways that tacit rules are tapped for and become visible in action and the ways that sensory experience can be understood to be culturally shaped. This conception reinforces the Durkheimian, 'strong programme' vision of culture as outlined by Alexander, and Alexander and Mast (as discussed in Chapter 3), albeit with an empirically oriented focus on practice and on informal learning (as described above through the example of faking like a woman, and Jackson and Scott's use of Becker's study of learning how to experience marijuana and its effects). Such a vision understands culture as (in Alexander and Mast's terms) a background condition of experience, something into which actors 'hook' their actions (and thus reveal themselves as types of actors).

Culture, in this perspective, is a backdrop for sense-making and for the figuring of action in the world. And action is performative enactment of underlying ('often unconscious' in Alexander's terms) scripts that culture provides. The actor or person can be seen to 'hook ... into' (Alexander and Mast, 2006: 1, quoted above) ways of being, talking and feeling that culture offers its actors and thus 'realises' (performs) a (what one assumes is 'the') social world. It is not possible to 'fall in love' or feel erotic, for example, without the available discourses with which such feeling forms are defined – the poetry and the accoutrements (see Chapter 9) through which 'love' has, at different times, been articulated, promulgated by commerce, as a recognisable cultural form ('this time', one might say to oneself, 'I am in love'). So too, it is not possible to *be* (or become) a man or a woman (recognisably) without hooking one's actions and experiences to kinds of background culture so that one's appearance, characteristics and actions come to be identified in socially *recognisable, patterned* ways – as instances of those more general categories. So too, as Durkheim described, it is not possible really to believe in a god without categories, rituals, practices and ways of seeing that hold fast that belief.

We are, in other words, *pulled* into forms of reality, whether as identities such as bi-polar, male, female, and as embodied feelings, such as being a *capoeira* exemplar, or being a heterosexual. And culture in this sense is 'strong'; it makes things seem meaningful, ordered and real; and in this sense then culture is enabling – cultural forms, once learned and internalised, empower us for action, perception and belief. And they empower some of us to do things to others in the name of what is good, beautiful and true.

It is easy, at this stage, to become taken up with what it is that culture can do and in the process to overstate the reality of culture and its powers. It is therefore worth taking a step back as I do in the next two chapters, to ask how much, and what kind, of a reality *is* culture? In asking this question it is also possible to consider how it is too simplistic to speak of culture in the singular or as a guiding, background scheme for action. What, then, about the shape of culture, its coherence, completeness and variation over time and space?

5

VARIATIONS IN SPACE AND TIME

So far, I have been speaking about 'culture' as if it were some stable entity, with boundaries around it and inflecting action and experience. But culture is, arguably, not that kind of thing; rather culture's own reality is more ambiguous, and more variable, more permeable and uncertain. In this chapter I consider the variability of cultural realities, over space and time. For, not only do cultural categories and practices vary geographically (nations, territories and regions, communities, groups, urban areas, tribes), they also vary temporally, both historically and micro-temporally in real-time, lived experience. There are and have been, in other words, many senses of reality. To introduce this theme, we can do no better than turn to the work of Mary Douglas and her focus on cleanliness versus dirt, the edible versus the inedible. As with Reed's study of the witches in Salem (described in Chapter 3), Douglas shows how 'dirt' is that which is out of place, that which stands out against culture's patterned background and thus calls for 'cleansing'.

CASE STUDY   Douglas on difference and things out of place, or blood and chocolate

Mary Douglas was arguably best known for her book entitled *Purity and Danger*. As Sara Delamont explains, 'the main contention in Douglas' most important book is summarized in her contention that "dirt is essentially disorder" and "dirt offends against order. Eliminating it is not a negative movement, but a positive effort to organize the environment"' (Delamont, 1989: 19). Thus, we take steps to maintain the places of things, physical, moral, symbolic. Thus, what is acceptable in one place may be seen as offensive, disruptive or otherwise polluting in another (reconsider Reed's discussion of the Salem 'witches'), and something that is out of place threatens to undermine symbolic

(Continued)

(Continued)

boundaries – our, as it were, what-goes-with-what-how orientation to reality, our realm of the real and thus our basis for cooperation, inter-subjectivity, order. Dirt, or pollution, is that which is 'out of place' or as Douglas herself puts it:

> Dirt is the by-product of a systematic ordering and classification of matter, in so far as ordering involves rejecting inappropriate elements. (2002 [1966]: 36)

As Delamont puts it, 'this basic idea, the centrality of classification as a source of personal stability, makes sense of many apparently bizarre customs reported from foreign parts. It also makes sense of many features of life in western industrialized societies' (1989: 20).

Consider, for example, a recent pudding featured on the menu of a highly regarded London restaurant. *Sanguinaccio* is concocted from, among other things, pig's blood and chocolate. Journalist Hugh Montgomery explains:

> As someone who equates dessert with dullness, I appreciate this one's frisson of danger: with your gorgeously glossy chocolate/marsala/vanilla/haemoglobin mix set to cook over a pan of simmering water for two hours, Kennedy ominously explains, it is 'vital to stir almost continually with a whisk or the blood will clot'. Thankfully, coagulation is avoided – credit to the slightly petrified vigilance of my sous chef Laura – and after chilling in the fridge for another couple of hours, the pâté is a perverse treat: just as you've been lulled into a false sense of chocolaty security, in comes the devilishly incongruous metallic aftertaste. My guests hesitantly agree it's good in small doses, with flavours evoked including 'mineral', 'bacon fries' and 'licking elbow scabs as a child'. (Montgomery, 2011)

The pudding confounds categories, drawing together things that seemingly 'do not go together' and that therefore seem dangerous and perhaps disgusting. The description of the pudding does so too, juxtaposing chocolate, metal, mineral, bacon and, perhaps the keynote, licking scabs. Indeed, the fact that this dish is classified as a pudding (a food category associated usually with comfort and security) rather than, say, a sausage flavoured with chocolate, enhances this food's 'dangerousness'. But its identity is also variable across space and time. In London, *Sanguinaccio* may gain cachet – where, for example, there are more diners who are or wish to be seen as daring or open-minded eaters – while in Naples the food is regarded as traditional. So too, when in parts of China, one might be encouraged to eat snake or boiled duck embryo but never fermented milk products (cheese) because the latter are disgusting.

Of course, within geographical boundaries, cities or nations there may be rival meaning systems such that what seems 'pure' to one group is 'dirty' to another. So, for example, carnivores in Exeter enjoy roast beef with Yorkshire pudding, while vegans in Exeter find that meal abhorrent. Or ahimsa fruitarians may be in conflict with vegans, eschewing not only meat, dairy, fish, eggs and grain but also vegetables that would not naturally fall to the ground (so no root, leaf or cruciferous vegetables). These differences highlight the topic of Chapter 7, namely that culture can offer multiple ways of fulfilling the sense of reality, the sense of what is natural, right or pleasant, for example.

The lines between purity, dirt, danger and disgust that are drawn not only vary across cultural space. They may also vary temporally, that is, over historical time and experiential, micro-time.

The first type of temporal change is relatively easy to grasp. To stick with the topic of food: diets change – London eel and pie shops are all but extinct circa 2014 (while possibly recipes containing blood and chocolate are on the rise); and the *Moosewood Cookbook* updated its 1977 vegetarian recipes in 2000 to cut down on cholesterol (Katzen, 2000). Returning to the performance of gender and sexual identity, the parameters of what it means to be 'womanly' change: those twin-sets with pearls that Agnes wore as emblems went out of fashion in the late 1960s and have been in and out of fashion since, as different understandings of femininity rise and fall. So too are there temporal variations in what counts as 'real' forms of illness.

CASE STUDY   Scott on the medicalisation of shyness

Since the 1950s extreme shyness has been transfigured. At one time considered to be 'cute' or 'endearing', this so-called character trait has emerged more recently as a form of phobia, a medicalised condition. Drawing on the work of Roy Porter (1997) and Bryan Turner (1995), Scott notes, 'various conditions enter and leave the realm of medical knowledge in line with changing ideas about socially desirable behaviour' (2006: 134). She continues:

> The stereotypical 'symptoms' of quietness, timidity and social withdrawal pose a significant challenge to the values of assertiveness, emotional literacy and vocal self expression that pervade

(Continued)

(Continued)

contemporary Western culture. Consequently, as shyness becomes less and less socially acceptable, the 'shyest' people are finding that their erstwhile deviant identities are being recast in biomedical terms and subjected to psychiatric treatment. (p. 149)

Scott sites this recasting process in pharmacology and the pharmaceutical industry, in genetic theories, in therapeutic clinics, counselling and cognitive behavioural therapy, and in the various discourses circulating within self-help manuals and other self-help resources. Her work highlights how social forms, images and categories – in this case pertaining to the culture of health and medicine – are produced by located groups and organisational actors, dramatised and elaborated as categories of experience. So as with bi-polar disorder, or femininity, individuals may find themselves located in these categories, in ways that are consequential. The categories are not 'given' but are themselves tuned and tailored; they have been subject, in other words, to historical change.

In this regard, Scott's focus on the ecologically shifting definitions of psychosocial conditions can be read as part of a wider shift in how mental health and illness is classified, and how increasing numbers of psychological conditions have come to be medicalised in ways that are linked to pharmacological forms of treatment. The recent publication of the fifth edition of the *Diagnostic and Statistical Manual* (the catalogue by which mental illness comes to be identified and classified) has been the subject of great debate. Looking at the ways in which this edition came to be drafted, revised, discussed and contested prior to publication (drafts were available online) highlights precisely how illness classification schemes are – to use the term from Walton and his discussion of the argument of the beard (Chapter 2) – conveniences.

The second type of temporality (variation within a category of being, reality as a variable signal) is equally important but perhaps not as fully explored by sociologists as it deserves to be. A day may be 'sunny' and yet at times clouds may pass. A social or political circumstance (being 'at war' or 'in conflict or struggle') or status identity (being 'in power' or 'in authority') may take on aspects that at times look like its opposite. Not every moment of a process or state of being is the same; time is, by contrast, heterogeneous. So, for example, despite 'being at war' with each other, during World War I on Christmas Day, German and British soldiers shared food and music, effectively enacting a truce (they resumed fighting the next day). So too, we speak sometimes about how we, as physical or aesthetic beings, are 'not always at our best' (a 'bad hair day' – see the Mary

Beard example discussed below and again in Chapter 6) or brightest ('I'm under par today'; 'I had a headache earlier') and we acknowledge, sometimes not in words, that there are times we are 'more ourselves' than others. We may utter these phrases without fully being aware of how this temporal variability may be so great that at times we wonder 'which me is the real me?' or 'was that me [saying, doing that]?' This variability may be related to physical matters (muscle tonicity, blood sugar, immune system, hormones, heart rate, blood pressure, electro-conductivity, water content, respiration, cellular activity and temperature all fluctuate according to rhythms and temporal events and circumstances) and it can be related to psychosocial matters (mood, emotion, arousal, motivation); all of these matters can interact, and provide conditions for each other. Even under circumstances where our social, psychological or physical conditions are at their seemingly most 'definite' (e.g., we are close to the end of life; we are in the pink of health), this variation can be observed or sensed.

CASE STUDY   DeNora on the variability of terminal illness

In work on music in everyday life at the end of life (DeNora, 2012), I have described how sociologists of health and illness seek to question the dichotomy of health 'versus' illness. I suggest that in terms of daily experience these categories are often blurred and indeed that most of us, most of the time, find ourselves hovering somewhere between health and illness (depending of course on how those terms come to be defined). The reality of health/illness, in other words, is much more nuanced and temporally variable than the binary notion of health/illness would permit; being 'healthy' or being 'ill' (and having the sense of being these things) is not to 'have' or be characterised either by an invariable physical state or by a consistent symbolic identity. Rather, I suggest, a more 'realistic' conception of health/illness is one that accommodates the mercurial 'nature' of health/illness conditions – how for example any 'illness' or, by contrast, state of health, will vary, not only along a continuum of 'good' and 'bad' times as the sociologist Kathy Charmaz has observed (1991), but also as varying senses of well-being (i.e., the sense of being well, irrespective of pain, decay or other 'negative' symptoms).

For example, as I have described (DeNora, 2012), even at the very last stages of life (amidst the suffering and physical disorganisation) there may still be 'good times', even if they are brief. They may result from the quantity or timing of pain medication, social interaction, time

(Continued)

of day, or many other matters. Indeed, some aspects of existence and social connection may be at their greatest during this extreme time (for example, connection to others and willingness to say the sorts of things one normally avoids). The question - and practical project - then becomes how to magnify the 'good times' and diminish their opposite, and just what does it take to craft situations so that this magnification may take place?

The temporal variation by which any, even the most extreme, health conditions come to be experienced may, as I suggested, be of as great a degree as the degree of difference between 'well' and 'ill' individuals. There is, in short, health within illness or 'intra-categorical' variation; there is no 'one' state of any form of illness. To the contrary, we need to consider the 'defining moments' of the swirling and varying and often-contradictory condition of 'health/illness'. And as with the phenomenon of illness, so too with any other form of category membership by which we delineate systems of acting, thinking, feeling, being: 'male/female-ness', 'delicious/disgusting', 'shy/bold', and many, many more. How particular features and temporally varying aspects of these identities are selected out and come to stand on behalf of a more general and more stable form of identity or reality situation is thus always of great interest to cultural sociology. We also need to ask how it is we come to latch on to these 'defining moments', these particulars that cause us to identify instances with categories.

So cultural categories structure what we come to count as reality; while this is not to say that the structuration process is in any way automatic or predetermined, cultural categories offer models for how to think about and experience realities. For now the key point is that what counts as 'real' and as 'the reality' of a situation, culturally speaking, will vary – over space and over historical time but also from moment to moment in real time. Thus, what counts as 'the' real situation, real identity or real condition is dependent upon, among other things (to be explored below), defining practices. These practices highlight some *aspects* of things as the 'important', 'real', definitive or 'true', aspects, while they suppress other aspects as irrelevant or inappropriate. Understandably, this process of defining is politically fraught. It may involve considerable acrimony and dispute.

To develop this theme I will now turn to a more extended case study, one that is centred around the question of physical beauty and physical decorum; more specifically, what counts as an appropriate look for someone (a woman, over 50) appearing on television. I will use this case study to consider the general matter of aesthetic conventions and their interrelation with aesthetically mediated entitlements. What looks 'right', in other words, and who, because of how they look, is entitled to do what with impunity? And how might all of this lead on to Wittgenstein's suggestion that 'ethics and aesthetics are one and the same' (*Tractatus*, 2001. 6.421)?

To explore these questions I now turn to a media controversy circa 2012–13 concerning the Cambridge Classics scholar and expert on ancient Rome, Professor (Winifred) Mary Beard. The controversy began after her appearance on a question-and-answer television programme called *Question Time*. (The programme invites a panel of well-known public figures to address topics of concern raised by members of a live audience. A note on data collection: I discovered this issue when it was reported in a national newspaper and pursued it as it continued to be discussed on the internet. I do not have or watch TV but have viewed relevant video clips on YouTube and BBC news sites. I don't know Beard but I am personally sympathetic to her situation during these years.)

CASE STUDY   A different kind of witch hunt?
The curious case of Professor Mary Beard

Mary Beard was often in the public eye circa 2012 as a television presenter of, among other programmes, *Meet the Romans* and *Pompeii: Life and Death in a Roman Town*. In January 2013 she took part in a BBC One broadcast of *Question Time*, a public-issues programme where notable figures are invited to offer answers to questions posed by members of the audience. One of her responses (on immigration) generated controversy among audience members, some of whom were vehemently against the points she made. She was thereafter subject to some abuse on various discussion lists.

On her own blog (Beard, 2013), Beard described how even her name came to be a source of ridicule and wonder:

> But why is it that people think that having a jibe at my surname is actually very interesting: she 'is in fact the twin sister of Tree Beard', '..I do not know whom Mary Beard is but wyth a name lyke that she surely hath a thyrd teat and a hairy clopper'; 'Am sure Mary Beard has a beard', :'A beardless wonder'; 'why does Mary Beard lack facial hair?'. And on and on ...

Some media columnists continued this abusive discourse, sometimes modulating it into a rant about Beard's appearance. In *The Spectator*,

(Continued)

(Continued)

for example, Rod Liddle (2013) suggested that Beard was only chosen to appear on TV because she has an 'eccentric' appearance and 'looks like a loony'.

Responses to Liddle's piece from readers further developed the theme, ranging from comments about her eccentricity, to how she looks like 'the bag lady just down the road' and 'like a nutter', to seemingly 'helpful' suggestions that she might wish to visit the tailor and hairdresser of one of the other participants in the Q/A television show, Anna Soubry, and also visit a dentist if she wishes to gain the 'respect' that her audience deserves.

Similarly, in a review of her programme on *Pompeii: Life and Death in a Roman Town*, A.A. Gill likened Beard's teeth to those of the corpses she was examining in the programme, and in a review of *Meet the Romans*, suggested that Beard was 'this far from being the subject of a Channel 4 dating documentary'. (The reference here is to a programme called *The Undatables* [*sic*] which seeks, as its website [*Undateables*] puts it – I shall return to this later – 'People living with challenging conditions are often considered "undateable" – this series meets a few and follows their attempts to find love' [quoted in Shea, 2012].)

THE POLITICS OF REPRESENTATION: PULLING TOGETHER THE STRANDS

Beard has described in print why she does not colour or style her hair in seemingly TV-friendly or gender-acceptable ways (her detractors fail to specify how she should alter her hairstyle), and why she doesn't wear makeup. She has actually described her own teeth as 'tombstone' teeth. She would appear to wear what look to be comfortable forms of clothing (loose, breathable) and – judging from video clips I have seen on YouTube of her television series on Pompeii – she wears sensible shoes. So what, exactly, is it with her critics?

Exploring the controversy around Professor Beard will help to direct us to the concerns that I will take up in Chapters 6 and 7 on reflexivity and multiple realities. For now, however, the Beard controversy is useful because it allows us to consider the following questions which I hope will draw together three related strands of the argument so far: (1) How does the 'case' of Mary Beard allow us to consider what Reed (also through an example of gender discrimination) calls the problem of 'too much' reality? (2) How does the example illustrate Douglas' argument about purity, dirt and danger (including an appreciation of how different cultures define these categories in different ways and a consideration of how women may be more prone to stepping 'out of line' than men)? and (3) How does the example highlight the matter of reality's temporal variation (as we saw earlier in the case of grave illness and its shifting moments of wellness/illness)? Pulling these strands together will begin to advance a more complex model of culture and how culture works, one that brings to the fore the 'mess' and interactional complication of how culture and action are inextricably entwined.

To turn to the first of these questions: by now, the reader will probably have been struck by the similarity of the 'witch hunts' that Reed described and some of the ways in which Mary Beard was persecuted by television 'critics', columnists and outraged members of the public. As with the witches in Reed's analysis, so too Professor Beard: cast against the foil of background assumptions of womanhood and televisual presence, Beard comes to be figured in the foreground as not blending in, as 'troublesome' in Judith Butler's sense.

The implication here is perhaps not unsurprisingly similar to the imagery that Reed describes in the Salem case. Along those lines, it is worth noting again that one writer who ridiculed her name (the gender-ambiguity of 'Beard' seemingly the prompt) also compared Beard with witch imagery, even using the 'olde' English spelling associated with the 17th-century times of the witch hunts ('wyth a name lyke that she surely hath a thyrd teat and a hairy clopper'). In both the case of the Salem witches and Beard (and others who are or might 'dare' to be like her), we are presented with women who stand out against the grain and so may seem to some observers to be in need of 'hunting' [sic] and 'removing' [sic], whether from our living rooms and TV screens (symbolic violence) or (physical violence) from our communities (17th-century Salem).

Turning now to the second question listed above, understanding Beard (or the witches) as 'out of place' points back to the work of Mary Douglas. That which offends, which is dirty or dangerous, is that which is out of place. Mary Beard's 'un-brushed' hair, and her long, *gray* hair, understood as an iconic feature of her general style, violates the quasi-sacred order of what is proper. To her detractors, her occupation of the slot of television presenter, looking as she does, defies a purported ethos (norms and imageries associated with an ethic) of who should be entitled to occupy this slot. Thus Beard's persona, her version of femininity, defies custom, is 'out of place' and thus is, in Douglas' sense, symbolically 'dirty'. (Had Beard been behind the tea urn at the Ladies Guild, digging in a garden or at an archaeological site, or presenting a gardening programme, or at home being 'a mum' or grandmum, her appearance might not have disturbed anyone.)

It could be argued that Beard's continued role in the public eye (more TV programmes despite her 'out of place' [sic] appearance [in Douglas' sense 'dirty']) queries the very assumptions and criteria against which she is judged. And the fact that Beard seems unabashed about all of this merely pushes this query to the forefront, drawing Beard (and ourselves as readers and judges) into the realm of representational politics (situation definition). It is a controversy over what can or should count as appropriate televisual appearance:

> I'm every inch the 57-year-old wife, mum and academic, half-proud of her wrinkles, her crow's feet, even her hunched shoulders from all those misspent years poring over a library desk ... I used to be scared of looking like this, but now I couldn't wish to be any different. Never mind the masochism of Botox, I can't even imagine dyeing my hair. It's not just the boring hours it would take. It's that every time you did it, you'd be reminded that you were hiding something. And how do you stop once you've started? (Beard, 2012a)

> Let's face it, I'm 58 and this is what I look like and, unless they've had an awful lot of expensive work done, this is what most normal 58-year-old women look like, too! (Quoted in Fryer, 2013)

So Beard is subjected to forms of chastisement because she has not engaged in – indeed she has resisted – forms of body-discipline deemed appropriate to the medium of TV. Beard retaliates by questioning the definition of that propriety. Unlike proponents of the Salem witch hunts, Beard's detractors do not for the most part seem to consider that she needs to be burned at the stake (though the threat of violence in some of the negative remarks she has received is, as she puts it, 'gobstoppingly misogynous'). Rather, at least for the most part, her detractors would appear to be calling for a more modern solution, i.e., the so-called 'total makeover' if Beard will persist in a media career.

Turning to the third question posed above, what of spatial, historical and temporal variation between the category of televisual attractiveness and instances of that category? Or in other words, surely Mary Beard is not monolithically 'ugly' all of the time, for all of the people in the world and worlds gone by? Considering spatial variation and the question, from Douglas discussed above, of what goes with what, where and when: might there not be some places in the world, or some enclaves in the UK, where Beard's appearance on TV might not seem out of place? (For example, in some parts of the world her appearance might be read as signifying elder-status and thus be deemed worthy of respect. And might not some people – perhaps those who dislike the look of dyed hair – find Beard's TV appearance actually pleasant or refreshing?) Considering historical-temporal variation, there were times in the past when gray hair was fashionable – the powdered wigs worn by European aristocrats, for example. Considering temporally changing appearance from moment to moment (the 'bad hair day'), a simple Google image search would suggest that Beard's (or anyone's) hair is not *always* dishevelled (or tidy-haired – the word dishevelled derives from the French word for hair), but that her appearance varies from day to day, moment to moment, image to image. So why should she be identified as someone perpetually dishevelled? Why, in other words, do images to the contrary get ignored?

MID-POINT STOCK TAKING

We have now arrived at a pivotal point in this book. I have been suggesting that reality (social, material, cultural) is complex but culturally simplified as it is distilled into cultural codes and categories (Chapters 1 and 2). I also considered this distillation as it can lead to violence and oppression (Chapters 1 and 3). I have described how culture can literally get beneath the skin (Chapter 4). In this chapter (Chapter 5), I have described how within cultures and across cultures there is variability in how realities are made manifest, and how even within a particular culture, the reality of a culturally mediated category is complex, mercurial, variegated in its day-to-day presentations, even when that category is something as seemingly definite as grave physical illness with its typical and attendant forms of suffering. In short, I have so far followed a neo-Durkheimian perspective (albeit one that is concerned with social performance or with, paraphrasing the title of Goffman's first book [1959], 'the presentation of social realities in everyday life'): that realities take on their characteristically real appearances through the ways that they are aligned with, and their perception is mediated by, interpersonal cultural categories, rules, images, concepts and, generally stated, meaningful forms. I have also alluded to the importance of materials and technologies in this mediation process, but so far they have played an adjunct role, like props, in this primarily social constructivist account which, in its emphasis of culture as a kind of mediating 'social fact', has also downplayed more 'Weberian' perspectives in which culture is understood to be both making of and made through meaningful action (Weber, 1978; Geertz, 1973: 5).

We are now at a point in this book where I hope that the importance of considering reality through 'how' questions is clear. By this I mean that we have seen that there is less point in asking 'what' something is (or indeed, what 'a culture' is) than in asking how things come to take on their apparent realities. More specifically, we have seen through the extended case study of the Professor Beard controversy how the matter of reality (e.g., situation definition) can be conflicted and, at times, unpleasant. We have considered how the question of who or what gains access to a category and thus reality status of a particular kind (who is insane, who is beautiful, who is male/female, who is a witch, what is edible) is negotiated. And we have considered how these categories vary spatially and temporally.

What we have *not* yet considered explicitly is the question of what kind of reality culture is, where it comes from and how it is itself formed and how that process involves, as I describe in the next chapter, a form of reflexive and enactive practice that draws instances and categories together in ways that define them both, simultaneously, in relation to each other. As we will see, this practice is simultaneously social and material – the categories cannot be severed and we will consider that point more explicitly in Chapter 8. First, though, we need to consider what is probably one of the more difficult points to be developed in the overall argument that I am making. It concerns the interrelation between culture in action and the question of what kind of reality culture is and how it gets defined.

6

REFLEXIVITY: ENACTING CULTURAL CATEGORIES *ALONG WITH* THEIR INSTANCES

Just what is the reality status of a cultural category, a rule or set of criteria? Culture does not sit in the background like a foil or defining medium against which instances are compared. As we have seen from the example of male/female, and again from the controversy around Mary Beard's 'appropriateness' for TV, cultural categories do not cover all contingencies; they are often ambiguous, flexible and in need of filling in. This is to say that culture as a reality is itself realised, created and made manifest through its invocation, and that is the point this chapter will develop.

Sticking for the moment with the example of Professor Mary Beard, and also sticking for the moment with a concept of culture as meaning-ful categories (which we will soon critique as an impoverished notion of culture), let's now up the stakes to consider a yet more controversial question. Might Beard's appearance not only be televisually appropriate but also 'beautiful' (beauty being understood as a general category of reality)? To gain precision, let's make this more specific and consider only Beard's hair – which so offended some television critics for being dishevelled and for being gray. Could it be beautiful?

As we shall see, there is a potential interplay between the meaning of what grayness is and Beard's entitlement to be aligned with the category of beauty. And these things can be tinkered with so that the former becomes justification for the latter (i.e., the very grayness becomes grounds for the reality claim of beauty). That tinkering involves a set of practices (I will later call these 'artful') whereby Beard, beauty and gray-ness are drawn together with other things, with, for example, metaphors, images, postures and people. This drawing-together involves action, and in ways that refract back on general categories, altering them in the process. Culture, in this case any preordained category of beauty, is, in itself, insufficient as a guide for knowing what the 'real' or 'right' judgement should be. Let's consider in more detail the question of what it is to be gray.

CASE STUDY   What *is* gray hair?

There is, one might suggest, no such thing as gray hair. Just as we saw previously that there is no such thing as the 'two-sex world', just as no two coke bottles are alike, so too there is no such thing as 'gray hair' versus other hair colours. Rather, there is silver, salt and pepper, platinum, gold, yellowy white, snow white, 'long silver fairy-queen kind of hair' (Warner, 2012), blue-gray, hydrangea, badger-like with stripes, multi-coloured and gray, and purple gray. One is reminded of the apocryphal legend of the Inuit many types of snow (which some have since suggested really only amounted to about five).

These metaphoric devices aid the appreciation of difference. They in turn also slow down thoughts/statements such as, 'That is gray hair so it must be unattractive' (note the word 'must'). And from this slowing, we can open up new possibilities for perception and interpretation through the ways that grayness is identified and linked to other categories, materials and practices (and their own reality statuses). In turn, it can forge different alliances to alternative values and scenarios. As such it is possible to re-value gray hair, and as a topic how this culturally innovative production takes place is of great interest: could it not be reconceptualised as brindled? Or lodged within a *wabi-sabi* aesthetic which values the natural, impermanent, the humble and 'the exquisite random patterns left by the flow of nature' (Juniper, 2003: 10). Could not gray hair resonate with the 'new perennial' movement in garden design ('dying in an interesting way is just as important as living' – Piet Oudolf).

The question of 'what' gray hair is takes us back, in other words, to Adorno's concern with material and with its handling, to his concern for being able to notice difference, and with expanding the perceptual grid so as to note this difference, the dissimilarity between things and the similarity between things that could be noted once we note these differences. So, how, in other words, can the formulation 'beautiful' be put together, with what interrelationship between form and content? For example, instead of being perceived as the lack of colour, the colour gray could be reappropriated as (just for example): natural silk, mother of pearl, iridescence, moonlight, silver, white gold, platinum, nickel, zinc, tree-bark, lake water, doves or diamonds (pairing it with categories of things that might be deemed valuable). It is possible, in other words, to reclaim gray hair, hypothetically, potentially, as beautiful (why not?!), a hair *colour* rather than the absence of colour, though this reclamation might have knock-on effects for how we think about other colours (is brown hair merely hair that has yet to turn white?). But in this reclaiming we are also tinkering with the forms that – conventionally, or so it is said – beauty 'must' take.

This, initially perhaps, trivial-seeming example is in fact linked to some far-from-trivial matters. It highlights what some scholars call 'lookism' (Warhurst et al., 2000, 2012) and the ways that lookism intersects with other forms of discrimination. Lookism is discrimination based on people's appearances and linked to the emergence of forms of work – in professional and service industries – that have become increasingly aestheticised and that imply employees who look and comport themselves in organisational-specific ways (Witz et al., 2003; Strati, 1999, 2008; Witkin, 1994, 2009). In the case of Professor Beard, lookism can be seen to overlap with beauty-based forms of age discrimination. In other cases, such as in the USA in the 1950s, hair aesthetics were often refracted through the prism of racial discrimination as this moving passage from *The Autobiography of Malcolm X* describes. (X is recounting what happened when he first agreed to a 'conk' – a home hair-straightening process):

> Shorty said … 'it burns *bad*. But the longer you can stand it, the straighter the hair' … I vowed I'd never be again without a conk … This was my first really big step toward self-degradation: when I endured all of that pain, literally burning my flesh with lye, in order to cook my natural hair until it was limp, to have it look like a white man's hair … to look 'pretty' by white standards. (Malcolm X, 2007 [1965]: 136–8)

As anyone who is familiar with Malcolm X's story will know, he did not, later on in his career, continue to believe that this 'relaxed' hair was beautiful, and abandoned the practice of trying to make it look 'like a white man's hair'. And Americans, increasingly during the civil rights movement in the 1960s, came to redefine canons of African American beauty: the 'Black is Beautiful' movement and the afro hairstyle were part of a celebration of – the creation of – a more inclusive set of aesthetic criteria for physical beauty.

In short, physical presence can, and without the need for words, challenge assumptions and values. By putting something in the 'slot' where we would normally not expect to see it, for example putting underarm or leg hair (see Chapter 2), unbrushed hair, gray or kinky hair in the slot where we expect beauty to be found, we challenge perception. Cultural categories and the realities they contain are by no means clear and by no means stable. There is no automatic identity between cultural categories and instances. Rather both are amenable to re-specification according to how they are combined, and this re-specification creates ambiguity which in turn permits us, as Mary Douglas writes, 'to enrich meaning or to call attention to other levels of existence' (Douglas, 2002 [1966]: 41).

Finally, we are ready to consider how the cultural realm, the realm that mediates our sense of what is 'real', itself gets reworked; how changes in reality are wrought. To move into this discussion let's continue with the category of beauty but turn now to a different example: urban geographical beauty and the case of seeing with 'parkour eyes'. This example will be used to further illustrate how there is a *mutual determination* (reflexive relationship) between instance and category and how it is out of this mutually determining relationship that the reality of aesthetic judgements can emerge. To put this differently, recognition is never passive but in fact is a way of renewing the meaning of, indeed enacting the reality of, categories, and thus of resetting the compass. To know 'what is what', in other words, is to make sense of reality. I will now develop this theme. At the same time I will now bring into the limelight the ways in which categories of meaning – including the things that we take to be good, beautiful and true – gain their 'reality' through the ways that meanings, practices and physical materials come to be aligned.

CASE STUDY   Seeing with parkour eyes

Parkour is the practice of moving smoothly and quickly across urban landscapes in ways that convert obstacles, such as walls, into stepping stones for movement. In a series of interviews with disciples of parkour Ameel and Tani (2012) describe how engaging in a practice can transform the ways that we judge the aesthetic appearances of things. Interpretation of the urban landscape is done through the medium of movement - does it afford good parkour (for example, good objects and materials for jumps and vaults), not is it 'pretty' in the terms that might correspond to some other evaluative discourse. Thus, the seemingly boring, purportedly 'ugly' concrete buildings that compose the urban landscapes of two Finnish cities (Helsinki and Jyväskylä) are, in relation to the practice of parkour, transfigured. They shift from being, as it were, non-places (i.e., not associated with people or activities, and evoking negative emotions), and grow beautiful because they are creatively interpreted against the ground of how they let one move. Thus, practices and uses of things or in relation to people can inform aesthetic criteria, and those criteria are illuminated as grounded aesthetics, that is, ultimately arbitrary and not autonomous. There is, in other words, no 'true' form of beauty but rather that category emerges in relation to situated practices and concerns. As the authors put it, traceurs:

> see walls, fences, rails, stairs and benches as opportunities that they can use in a creative and playful way (see also Lam, 2005). Often, environments and materials which are usually interpreted as boring, banal and even ugly are appreciated among traceurs as ideal environments for parkour. But going beyond the appreciation of mere surface materials and textures, parkour also shows a new kind of interest in architectural features and choices in the way traceurs evaluate their environment. This evaluation happens both on the basis of usability and of aesthetic values; traceurs continuously stress the idea that an interesting environment should allow for different types of uses (see also Brown, 2007). (Ameel and Tani, 2012: 169).

Those practices can, the authors describe, 'open up new perspectives on everyday surroundings':

> After the traceurs had their 'parkour eyes' opened, they started to look at their environment in a new way. Places that had not attracted their attention before began to show interesting and attractive features, and the traceurs started to attach new meanings to their environments. 'Parkour eyes' is not only about seeing possibilities in unexpected places, but also about seeing possibilities for attaching new and unexpected feelings to a place. Seen with such eyes, spaces that had been largely detached from links to history or location become inscribed again with an appreciation of their symbolic significances and their identity. By developing an embodied relation with largely inauthentic environments or non- places, traceurs gradually create, by way of their embodied activities, what amounts to a more authentic sense of place (see Relph, 1976). (Ameel and Tani, 2012: 170)

One simply 'sees things' in different ways and this seeing has evolved from a form of doing and the continuous search for good sites for that doing. The case study of parkour eyes thus shows us how, really, anything

(Continued)

(Continued)

can be beautiful. Beauty is in the eye of the beholder but that eye is in turn focused through specific forms of cultural practice and their connection to materials. That practice provides the grounds for a grounded aesthetic that transfigures 'ugliness' such that it is perfectly possible for Jyväskylä to be more beautiful than Venice.

In sum, if we allow Beard (or Jyväskylä) to pass into a category that is otherwise restricted (in this case beauty), that passage *instantiates* the formula or category; it renews that form such that when it is next upheld, it may have altered its shape, may be applicable in new ways and thus help us to appreciate and perhaps do new things. By allowing new instances to try on categories we stretch those categories to fit (be known through) those instances and this is part of what it means to speak of cultural innovation. Indeed, as Adorno described, this is what music could do (we could here speak of the arts and aesthetic media more generally): it re-sensitises, offers potentially new possibilities for perception and experience. As I will explore in Chapter 8, if we cannot 'see' the beauty in Beard, Jyväskylä or (fill in the blank here), it is because the lenses through which we happen to be using in order to view those things are ones that direct our attention to some things and away from others, and this (mis)direction is a form of selective inattention.

REFLEXIVITY

We are now at the place where we can begin to appreciate more fully the complex, dynamic interrelationship between cultural categories, classes, identities, slots or rules (general things) and specific, actual, particular examples, people, characteristics or events that come to count as (real) instances of those general things. I have so far used the example of beauty (which probably most people would think has more 'wiggle room' than, say, an example that dealt with the reality status of something physical or material) to show how categorical definitions – concepts of general realities – are far from clear, far from stable but, rather, are inherently ambiguous, plastic and emergent. I will return later on to consider other, so-called 'harder' realities such as, in Chapter 7, physical disease, Chapter 8, the sensation of pain and in Chapter 9, the reality of disability.

For now, the point I wish to make is this: if we persist in thinking of culture as a map (the deeper structures that inform the surface acts), it is probably useful to think of that map as rendered in low resolution. It is certainly not an Ordnance Survey account of every contour of a culture (a complete taxonomy), let alone a GPS system with a code-generated voice that tells us when to turn or how to move. To navigate, in other words, not only do we often need to rely upon our, often improvised, locally honed devices but also – as I will describe – simultaneously our navigation 'discovers' and creates the cultural terrain that purportedly was there 'already'. To put this differently, unlike hill walkers armed with map and compass, as cultural actors we make the cultural maps that we act as if we are merely following. This is to say that formal realities such as beauty or disability, health and illness need to be understood as *emerging* in relation to the practices through which their senses, and their locational, relational identities, are made apparent. This point now needs development.

To speak of this work of linking instance to category is to speak of the reflexive relationship between the here and now and the there and then. Our conscious awareness of this kind of reflexivity may, however, be more or less acute. One may, for example, genuinely believe that the matching of instance to category, action to code, is effectively automatic and so remain unaware of the 'work' one does to achieve this apparent alignment. Recall, for example, Garfinkel's Agnes: in seeking to pass as a natural, normal female, she was, perhaps, overly obsequious to a set of criteria and a cultural image. Unlike Mary Beard, whose appearance either deviates from or (if we declare her beautiful) modifies the category of beauty (as articulated by the TV critics and others discussed above), Agnes studiously sought to align herself with what she took to be pre-existing notions of the category of femininity. And yet, that very studiousness about the rules and codes (as if they could ever be followed in full) offered object lessons in what those rules and codes seemingly specified, namely what a feminine woman looks and acts like. (Agnes was, readers might say, acting like a cultural dope in relation to the criteria of femininity. She could have questioned those criteria but instead sought to follow them religiously. Perhaps this devotion to 'the rules' was linked to Agnes' awareness of her ambiguous gender identity [revealed in a follow-on to Garfinkel's text] – perhaps Agnes wished to ensure that there would be 'no question' of her femininity and that a 'twin-set and pearls' version of femininity could protect her gender identity against doubt.)

That seemingly 'clear' ideal of femininity to which Agnes oriented does not, I suggest, exist, or at least not in the unambiguous sense that Agnes' actions would seem to imply. First, there is more to passing as feminine than the mere 'wearing of twin-sets and pearls'. There are other, more refined aspects of this 'rule' which could continually be unravelled ('What sort of shape is the body in the twin-set?', 'How does one move when wearing a twin-set?', 'When should one not wear a twin-set?', 'What colour twin-set', etc.). Similarly, one might imagine a way of wearing those sweaters that was too 'formal', too 'careful' (but of course, who pronounces this?) in ways that could be said to demonstrate a form of 'trying too hard' to look appropriately feminine (think of Jack Lemmon and Tony Curtis in *Some Like It Hot*, or Dustin Hoffman in *Tootsie*). Once we begin to delve into the question of *what counts as the rule* (e.g., how to be orthodoxly feminine) we discover yet more rules to be clarified, and behind them, yet more unclear rules (one could imagine a rule whereby this 'over-careful' look was considered desirable and 'most' feminine!). There is, in short, no formal way to complete the quest for complete criteria, complete instructions, because the reality of the rule lies in its instantiation, in its practical enactment, here and now as we draw things together so as to make sense of the kind that either says or implies, '*This* is *that* and *that* is *this*'.

INDEXICALITY

So, for example, if you say to me, 'Beard is not beautiful' or 'Beard could not be beautiful', I might say, 'Why not?' To which you reply, 'Because beauty involves looking groomed and it involves having hair that looks youthful.' And then I say, 'But what about So-and-So, they appear on TV with messy (or gray) hair.' And you say, 'Yes, but that is a different type of messiness/urban aesthetic.' I then say, 'But how do you mean "different"?' And you say, 'Well, it is a style known as "the beach hair look".' And I say, 'But why isn't this gray, uncombed hair an example of the beach hair look?' To which you reply, 'Well it doesn't work with gray hair.' And I then say, 'But why is blond ok, but gray not?' and you reply, 'blond is a *colour*; gray is faded from another colour.' But then I say, 'But surely blond is not a colour either but a faded version of light brown?' (So far, I am still restricting the discussion to examples of how cultural categories are instantiated through verbal utterances – later we will see that meanings come to be asserted and sometimes made intractable by their relation to material and embodied practices.)

We could continue, as this example highlights, *ad infinitum*, in an attempt to specify what, ultimately, may not be specifiable (at some point exasperation would probably set in and we would stop, agreeing to disagree). In the end you say, 'Well never mind, if you can't see the difference, there's no point in continuing to talk about it!' On that point, you are right because (a) the terms that define beauty can never be fully spelled out and (b) we seem to have incommensurate definitions of what 'beauty' might mean. And so we discover that terms really only come alive, take on meaning, through the ways they are instantiated, when in practice, we link an example to the category it exemplifies. You and I cannot agree because we are instantiating the term 'beauty' with incommensurate – or so we believe – examples (apples and oranges rather than types of apple, but then, what counts as an apple anyway?).

This ambiguity is known as *indexicality*: the essential impossibility of ever fully specifying in the abstract what it is that a rule or set of criteria can mean because each clarification brings with it yet more to clarify. The inherent ambiguity that the concept of indexicality points to is a feature of all rules, meanings and categories. That ambiguity can be resolved in only one way – through action, that is, through the linking of general criteria to specific instances. And to speak of action is to speak of contexts of use. In fixing meaning we cut the Gordian knot of the endless ambiguity involved in knowing whether or not 'this' is an example of 'that'. Instead we fuse 'this' and 'that' through our cross-cutting acts of recognition, of rule-following. Thus to varying degrees, rule-following is always rule-making.

So, for example, if 'we all agree' that Beard, or Jyväskylä, is beautiful, we do not attempt to unpick or dispute whatever it is that we think we mean by the term beauty (or if we do we are asking for trouble, seeking to open up that which we, or some of us, wish to keep closed). We are *acting as if* that category were plain as a pikestaff; we let the potential contradiction pass. We act as if our recognition of Beard, and our aligning her with the category of beauty, were easy, unproblematic: *anyone* would know how to see this, we might say. And yet, that recognition may involve highly creative forms of practice that make the category fit the instance. We may not even realise that we are engaging in such practices when we say things like 'gray hair is the colour of moonlight' until someone else comes along and says, 'Don't be stupid, it's the colour of rags and old iron!' When our tacit assumptions are challenged, when we find that the indexicality of a category allows others to see things differently, our presumed reality is breached and conflict may ensue. But in the breaching we also reveal what it takes to produce these realities or, as Garfinkel puts it (note that this is the first time I have mentioned Garfinkel's term 'artful practices'):

> [e]very feature of sense, of fact, of method, for every particular case of inquiry without exception, is the managed accomplishment of organized settings of practical actions … particular determinations in members' practices of consistency, planfulness, relevance, or reproducibility of their practices and results – from witchcraft to topology – are acquired and assured only through particular, located organizations of artful practices. (1967: 32)

FINITISM

The idea that sense-making is contingent upon contexts of action, and that sense-making is produced in and through action, is an idea that emphasises the indexicality of meanings and rules. It is sometimes called the doctrine of 'finitism' when it is discussed in the philosophy of science. A finitist position understands that the recognition of rules, and thus the maintenance of categorical realities, are dependent upon the contingent, situated 'work' of making sense in practice (Barnes, 1982). Practice is not the manifestation, in surface action, of 'deep' rules; it is the instantiation of what comes to count as 'the rules'. This means, as Heritage has put it, that:

> Categories are maintained or altered entirely through the accumulation of individual acts of judgment and their acceptance (or rejection) by other members of a language community. (1984: 146–7)

In passing, it is important to note that with these words, Heritage does not mean the judgements of individual *people* but rather that meaning emerges retrospectively through the accumulation of enactments over time. The direction of history, even less so progress, is not, in other words, preordained (for example, as Whig histories of scientific progress might imply). Its plotted course could have been otherwise and is at least potentially negotiable in each and every one of its coordinates over time. And as we will see, this notion of emplotment includes materials – objects, tools, aesthetic media: it is by no means achieved merely through the modality of talk. (This point highlights the implicit but never-fully explicit piece of the puzzle that classical ethnomethodology did not explore, which was later picked up and made central to ethnomethodologically informed work in science studies and organisational interaction; see Chapter 7.) So, for example, the frequent appearance of well-groomed women (or rather women who make use of beauty-industry products) on television recurrently enacts an image of an 'appropriate' TV-look, just as the culture devoted to appreciating Venice (via the Turner and Canaletto paintings, the novels by Hemingway and Henry James, the memoirs by Goethe, the BBC television series and the tourist industry) enacts or repeats the reality of that city's beauty by offering myths and legends (object lessons) on how to make sense of the city's 'essential' beauty. In both cases, the authority of these realities can be queried 'next time around' and in ways that gain traction through repetition and through repeated demonstration (more Mary Beards on TV, for example, or attempting to see Venice through 'parkour eyes').

As a perspective on how knowledge is produced, finitism implies attention not to 'what' things are but rather to 'how' they come to be recognised and agreed upon. And this attention is devoted to what Garfinkel called the 'artful practices' by which this work is achieved. Artfully, for example, I you we craft a narrative, paint a picture, display ourselves, perceive some set of stimuli, so that I, you, we can recognise some aspect of reality, so that we can organise the world *conveniently* in patterned ways, and so that we can find a way to connect with each other. Thus, the study of culture must include the artful, crafty, often-playful practices by which the work of representing the world 'as if' it pre-exists this work is conducted. The term 'artful' reminds us in turn of an early meaning of the word 'culture', as cultivation or the tending of crops, or as preparing and making (Williams, 1976: 87–93). It reminds us, in other words, that cultural sociology needs to consider its subject as a verb as well as a noun. One can, for example, culture tastes, intellectual faculties and bacteria. Thus culture is *both* the medium within which realities are made manifest and the artful practices by which this occurs and, in making sense of reality, all social actors are creative workers, artists or, again in old-fashioned parlance, 'makers' as in Giambattista Vico's (1668–1744) sense as Witkin describes it: 'the only things of which one can be said to have true knowledge or understanding are those things which one has made oneself' (Witkin, 2003: 4).

Thus to pose what some might call an unconventional question (such as, Could Mary Beard [or Jyväskylä] be beautiful?) is to illuminate both what is at stake when cultural incongruities or breaches are asserted. It is to highlight the ways in which the inclusion of incongruities widens the lens of what can be seen and accommodated within cultural forms. It is perfectly possible to develop a category of beauty that includes, for example, the old as well as the young, the gray as well as the blond. Indeed, thereafter it is possible that previous categories of the human-beautiful may be perceived to have been impoverished. Hence culture undergoes change from within and in incremental ways that are less dramatic but perhaps more powerful and enduring than the gestalt shifts we normally think about when we speak of cultural paradigms and revolutions.

We are now halfway through this book *and only now at the starting place* of what the investigation of everyday reality can offer, and what it should include. That is, we can now turn to the project outlined by John Law who has observed: 'Every time we act or tell, we also, at least putatively, make a difference. We always act politically. The only question is how do we do it?' (Law, 2002: 7). What kinds of artful practices are involved when cultural categories are instantiated and exemplified, when events, people and situations are lodged, for all practical purposes, under the banner of categorical identities?

This focus on practice, on actual attempts to make and state the world, takes us into a form of cultural sociology that moves us beyond the neo-Durkheimian concern with cultural structures. It draws us into what some, taking inspiration from Stoller (1997), have called 'sensuous scholarship' or 'research about the human senses, through the senses, and for the senses' (Vannini et al., 2010: 378). It requires a mode of enquiry that not only thinks, but looks (listens, touches, tastes, smells), to elaborate on Wittgenstein as quoted above. Such a perspective entails painstaking work; it is where 'slow sociology' comes into its own. That means considering how certain effects, events, sensibilities, situations, identities and sensations are produced and experienced – multi-modally – in daily life.

CULTURAL SOCIOLOGY AND METHODOLOGY

As I have said, cultural sociology's greatest power is its emphasis on the ways in which reality is culturally mediated and re-mediated (over time and place), and in ways that 'get into' action, embodiment and experience. We have seen how culture facilitates concerted action, how it provides the basis for intersubjectivity (or what we take to be intersubjectivity). We have also seen the 'darker' side of culture, how culture can be dangerous, offering 'too much' reality. We have, in short, every reason to adopt a 'strong' or robust theory of culture in action. The question, then, is how to theorise cultural complexity and how to investigate culture in action.

Proponents of the 'strong programme' have taken us a long way toward understanding how reality comes about. They advocate an investigative and explanatory focus on the ways in which what comes to be taken to be 'real' is formulated. This focus has been directed to cultural images, models, discourses, categories, classes, procedures, scripts and arrangements of symbols, and this focus is linked to a methodology that is interpretive and descriptive of the symbolic systems or frameworks that produce reality.

As Reed describes this methodology, cultural sociology 'must push beyond the surface reports of actors and the immediate meanings available in the investigator's evidence to grasp some deeper set of meanings that inhere in the action under study' (Reed, 2011: 10). With these words, Reed would seem to adopt the sociological tradition of understanding action and agency in relation to structures outside individuals. This tradition downplays individual free will and its concomitant methodological individualism in favour of perspectives that understand individual action and experience as formulated in and through reference to things outside the individual and between individuals.

This programme is laudable. It quite rightly refuses to locate identities or conditions 'in' individuals, an issue to be explored in Chapter 9. But its antidote to individualism involves, via Durkheim (and Lévi-Strauss), a sociological form of psychoanalysis (as Alexander put it – see Chapter 3), an excavation of culture's deep structures, rather than a focus on the production histories (longer and very short term in the here and now) of how cultures are made, stabilised and changed. In keeping with the focus on indexical cultural structures, and with the finitist perspective described above, I propose a more symmetrical focus on how action and culture are mutually determining (a focus that does not require deep digging in order to locate culture's structuring powers) and one that does not reduce culture merely to the acts of individuals.

Methodologically, this focus benefits from the study of controversy or rival attempts to make sense of reality. It does not privilege anyone's account of how action came about. It does not privilege participant accounts because it understands these as cultural productions and thus as artistic products, as acts in their own right, not words 'about' acts. For the same reasons, it does not privilege researchers' accounts about what is going on, or what things mean. Indeed, from within the focus I am proposing, attempts to explain surface action through reference to some set of underlying structures – categories of action, scripts, classification systems and rules – is not merely insufficient; it is a form of activism, one that reflexively performs the realities it purports merely to describe. Finally, the focus I propose is not 'micro' analysis, if by that we mean the study of what individuals do and say, as opposed to something bigger, for example the study of 'larger forces' behind the scenes. To the contrary, we need to avoid the micro–macro divide (another false dichotomy!). On this point the work of Bruno Latour has been illuminating.

Latour speaks persuasively of what he terms the 'dead alley' where organisations (cultures) are construed 'as sui generis meta- or macro-entities "inside" which social theorists always try to put the little, puzzled, limited human actors as if they were another doll in another Russian doll' (2011: 175). Latour goes on to suggest that instead of the metaphor of the nested dolls, we consider something 'flatter' whereby no set of structures, no context, can be presumed *a priori* but rather a metaphor in which all contexts and constraints are enacted and thus asserted through the drawing-together, the enfolding of people and things, and allusions to rules, so as to make a semblance (a sense) of reality, and in ways that side-step the virtual/real dichotomy. This way of thinking about and looking at social life and its realities has affinities with what is sometimes called figurational sociology (Gabriel and Mennell, 2011), in which evolving or forever 'dancing' networks of humans, objects and practices are understood in terms of how they 'figure' or constitute worlds. (It also resonates with the 'figured worlds' approach of Holland et al., 1998.) It considers the places, as Gary Alan Fine describes it, where the action is (Harrington and Fine, 2006; Fine 2010), namely situated, temporal and collaborative forms of action or the drawing-together of people, meanings and things. When we do that, what is there for us to see and how?

To sum up, cultural sociology will not be strong if it conceptualises action and agency as a matter of individual volition – we know this from previous articulations of the 'strong programme'. It will also not be strong enough if it leans toward the opposite of this false dichotomy and prioritises cultural 'structures' (categories, rules, frames, scripts, codes) as the sources of actors' motivation, energy and lines of conduct (as if the play were pre-scripted sufficiently that actors did not have to co-author their lines and moves). Cultural sociology can be made even stronger if it considers the zero-hour of artful practices where culture and action are conjoined. Culture, in other words, is not an explanatory resource but a topic for cultural sociology.

This point is well-recognised in cognitive anthropology. For example, as Charles Frake puts it, '[c]ontext is not there to be seen. Its specification is a social accomplishment' (1997: 38). Similarly, Wieder (1971) has described how everyday language use is open-ended to the extent that it is:

> inappropriate to conceptualize its use in terms of a rulelike semantics. That is, in everyday talk persons constantly use expressions the sense of which is relative to the place in which it is spoken, what the hearer knows about the speaker, the time at which it is spoken, and an indefinitely extendable collection of other contextual matters. (1971: 108)

In subsequent work, Wieder (1974) describes how telling about the rules of culture, language or some 'code' of conduct (such as inmates' code of conduct while in prison), whether as researcher or research subject, is simultaneously fabricating the reality of culture and specific instance. These perspectives complement but also re-specify the Durkheimian tradition as I described in the Preface to this book. That is, they show how the very notion that reality is 'out there' and a given to be discovered is itself a resource for its reflexive production in the here and now as alignments between 'this' instance and 'that' category are drawn and consolidated. They reconceptualise the relationship between culture and action, allowing for mediated contingencies of action, which is an understanding that culture is itself subject to active 'filling in' through actions that refer to and mobilise culture. Culture, then, like experience, like situation, like interest, is itself an emergent object, performed and defined in and through situated actions lodged under its auspices. Culture is line drawing *but* its lines are *drawn from within situations of action*.

How that artful practice takes shape, how alignments are made between categories and instances that define each in relation to the other, is cultural sociology's topic. That topic includes a focus on the attendant features of situations that produce or bring resolution to otherwise ambiguous phenomena, making them 'seem like' some category of reality. And it includes creating situations that draw together practices, categories and objects so as to structure perception in ways that enhance versions of what can be perceived while suppressing perceptions that detract from other reality claims. Is it any wonder that John Law (2004) describes this process as 'mess'?

How, then, to combine a theoretical commitment to cultural mediation and culture's causal properties with a methodological stance that does not overplay culture's mediating role? And how to avoid a conception of culture as unified (e.g., 'our' culture in the UK)? How to retain space for ambiguity and multiple understandings of culture's content and – importantly – conflict over different readings and renditions of 'our' culture? There are, in other words, multiple possibilities in culture – renditions, strands and even contradictory codes. Thus, to the problem of, as Reed put it, 'too much reality' we need to add the additional problem of multiple or 'too many' realities.

7

MULTIPLE REALITIES AND THEIR MAINTENANCE

As an entry into the issue of multiple realities, consider numerous 'faithless' or multiple readings of any published text – Durkheim's own, for example. As Alexander and Smith have noted (2005: 2), Durkheim's texts are incapable of fixing any one hard-and-fast reading, even among scholars who devote hundreds of hours to fine-grained interpretation. To the contrary: debate, controversy, different readings and rival representations of what Durkheim meant abound.

As with Durkheim's books, so too the symbolic forms that structure our acts and consciousness: culture does not in itself underwrite or contextualise or frame actions and perceptions. Culture is not, in other words, an explanatory resource of social action but is, along with action, a topic to be explained.

Thus, as we have just explored in Chapter 6, the question of making sense of reality includes the ways in which categorical meanings offer broad and elastic canopies that can be shaped in myriad ways (e.g., there is more than one way to speak in French; to be a son, a sister or a citizen; to be a man or a woman, male or female, beautiful or ugly). Social forms, then, understood as the cultural circumstances within which we make our realities, are themselves amenable to multiple meanings, multiple appropriations. We are ready now to consider the idea of multiple realities.

Alfred Schutz (1945) was one of the first social theorists to broach this idea. He described the idea of multiple realities in terms of the different provinces of meaning that constitute our experience – the paramount reality of the world of work (the everyday reality where we operate) and the other provinces of reality such as dream, theatre and religious experience. We may, for example, experience alternation as we awake from what – as we tune into the working reality – we recognise as 'only a dream'. Though Schutz did not explicitly develop the point, it is also possible to consider the ways in which our working, waking realities are themselves multiple, that is, capable of multiple interpretations.

Karl Heider (1988) described this problem as the 'Rashomon Effect' which refers to situations in which ethnographic accounts about 'a culture', the customs and meaning systems associated with a particular place, contradict each other. The focus on contradictory accounts also serves to underline how the exercise of decoding action, or attempting to reveal the ur-texts (the 'formulations') that guide action is by no means straightforward, no matter how careful, adept and nuanced the reader (recall the discussion of indexicality in Chapter 6). Heider poses the question, how can we resolve disagreements about which is the 'correct' or valid interpretation? His 'charter image' is taken from the 1950 Kurosawa film, *Rashomon*. Based on two short stories by Ryunosuke Akutagawa, the story explores four divergent eyewitness accounts of one event. Each account is presented as 'the true' account of the event and there is no resolution at the end of the film – the viewer is left in a state of uncertainty.

Heider's answer is that just as there is no one 'objective' account of an event or situation, so too there is no 'one' way to interpret a culture's typified meanings and thus how a culture comes to structure action, perception and the recognition of reality. We need therefore to take a step back from a concern with events and culture's structure, and think instead about whether the assumption that there is a shared reality, a shared culture that formulates shared reality, might nonetheless allow for widely divergent instantiations of those formulae. There may, in other words, be opposing strands within cultures – just as with languages there are dialects and divergent usages. So for example, and in keeping with the topic of variation considered in Chapter 5, Heider suggests that differences of interpretation may be due to factors such as regional, temporal and situational differences in cultural understanding. Cultures change, and are subject to variation over time and place. So, too, coming at the reality of cultural texts from different perspectives and different locations or roles will deliver varied results.

But Heider's article, despite its revelation of the possibility of the ethnographic Rashomon Effect, remains committed to the technical details that impede reliable interpretations of culture. In this regard, his conception of culture is still one in which culture is an object to be known, and once known, a resource that can explain action. He does not consider how culture is itself enacted through the ways that it is instantiated (as discussed in Chapter 6). We need, in other words, to understand culture in terms of how culture, or rather assertions about reality as formulated in culture, may not suit all of the instances that would otherwise seek to enact cultural categories, which is to say that identifications between instances and the categories that are said to define them may be disputed, be perceived as alien or enigmatic. Consider Durkheim again on the relationship between the individual and language:

Indeed, there are hardly any words, even among those we commonly use, whose meanings do not to some extent surpass the limits of our personal experience. A term often expresses things we have never perceived, experiences we have never had or never witnessed. Even when we know some of the objects which it concerns, it is only as particular examples that serve to illustrate the idea which they would never have been able to form by themselves. *Thus there is a great deal of knowledge condensed in the word which I never collected, and which is not individual; it even surpasses me to such an extent that I cannot even completely appropriate all its results. Which of us knows all the words of the language he speaks and the entire signification of each?* (Durkheim, 2001 [1912]: 330, emphasis mine)

WHOSE REALITY? MAPPING THE SPEECH COMMUNITIES AND THEIR CULTURAL POLITICS

Thus in addition to the notion that culture encodes and presents reality, we need the notion that within any given social realm, space or network, realities will be differentially shared, differentially instantiated and differentially understood. Thus it is problematic to speak of 'a' group's culture or 'a' lens through which a social group perceives. Instead, it is perhaps more useful – and here a cue can be taken from Max Weber's highly nuanced work on comparative religion, including his discussion of the variegated forms that Protestantism assumes – to consider heterogeneous (tangled, cross-cutting, variably textured) spaces and processes of reality production and invocation. Such a conception of culture lifts the symbolic canopy just a bit higher to let us examine the currents and cross-currents of symbolic production that are part of the simultaneous, or reflexive, enactment of instance and category. The method for this scrutiny is the observation of conflict, breakdowns and other types of cultural 'trouble'.

> **CASE STUDY** Luker on *Abortion and the Politics of Motherhood*
>
> In a 1984 book that became an instant classic, Kristin Luker set out to explore the question of how it happens that the unborn fetus is, on the one hand a collection of cells or, on the other, a small baby waiting to
>
> *(Continued)*

(Continued)

be born. Of course, how the fetus is identified is connected to many other important concerns, among them the question of a woman's right to terminate a pregnancy.

As Luker put it, '[m]uch as the slavery question once did, the abortion issue polarizes ... Why is the debate so bitter, so emotional? Part of the answer is simple: the two sides share almost no common premises and very little common language. For example, those who oppose abortion usually begin by stipulating that since the embryo* [Luker here explains why she chose this term] is an unborn child, abortion is morally equivalent to murder. But for those who accept abortion, this initial stipulation is exactly what is problematic; from their point of view, the embryo has the capacity to become a child but it is not a child yet, and it therefore belongs in a very different moral category. Thus, one side begins with a given that the other side finds highly debatable, that the embryo is the moral equivalent of the child it will become' (pp. 1–2).

Luker describes how, for people who are deeply involved in the abortion issue, 'these differences of opinion, and the inability to have anything resembling a dialogue about them, are not serious problems. They dismiss those who disagree with them as being either ignorant of the facts or perversely unwilling to admit the truth when it is presented to them' (p. 3).

In keeping with the interpretive perspective outlined by Alexander and Smith, by Alexander, and by Reed, Luker shows how it is not 'the facts' that are at stake but, rather, what the facts are taken to mean, how they come to be lodged (lifted) in cultural meaning systems where they gain clarification. Thus, the fact that a fetus has a heartbeat, but cannot breathe, is taken by pro-life advocates to mean that it is a person who 'in time' will be able to breathe (respiration is unimportant). Conversely, for pro-choice advocates, all babies breathe, thus the inability to breathe indicates that the fetus is not a baby. As Luker puts it, '[t]he two sides therefore examine exactly the same set of "facts" but come to diametrically opposed conclusions about them' (p. 5).

It is likely that the clear bifurcation of opinion that Luker describes offers an unusually heightened case of how realities can be diametrically opposed. In this case, the starkly opposed conceptions of 'the fetus' may be understood to derive from the kind of respondents Luker interviewed, as she herself points out: because these interviewees were key activists in the public debate over abortion rights, taking a clearly defined stance and remaining consistent were both necessary and an aim. They were positioning themselves for or against a single issue and thus seeking to achieve textual and practical unequivocality. In everyday life, where battle lines are less sharply drawn, and around issues where much less may be at stake, it is possible to see a much higher degree of vacillation and indeterminacy, the invocation of competing codes and discourses and moment-to-moment contradiction. Nonetheless, realities emerge in relation to the ways they are encoded, but there is more than one (bioethical) code and more than one way of constructing the basis of personhood in operation in American society today.

Luker's book would probably be read by the advocates of the strong programme as still too instrumentalist because she seeks to situate discourses about the personhood/non-personhood of the fetus in relation to vested interests and, more significantly, to 'states of social reality – states that they find reassuring or threatening' (p. 7), to worldviews that simultaneously spell out pragmatic life arrangements, such as how women's reproductive roles connect to other roles, for example in the workforce. In this sense, her understanding of culture is culture as a 'tool' and values and beliefs understood, in Bennett Berger's terms, 'ideological work', or (Berger was investigating childrearing practices and ideals among rural communards) the tailoring of convictions to circumstances and interests (Berger, 2003 [1981]: 18). Another way of looking at this tailoring, however, is to suggest it is the result of the need to make culture more bespoke, to make categorical values, ideals, images and definitions (meanings) fit the places where one is, the things that one can do and entertain. If culture is script, or even if culture is fragmented script, then action is the adaptation of that script to make it actionable, habitable for and by us, here and now. What is 'good childrearing'? What 'is' the thing that some people call the fetus and others call the baby?

PHYSICAL REALITIES ARE MULTIPLE TOO

It is here that a concept from science studies – the 'boundary object' – is helpful. It takes us a bit further away from arguments about how to define things into a focus on artful practices. A boundary object is something – idea, object, form of disease – that is, as Star and Griesemer (1989: 393) put it:

> both plastic enough to adapt to local needs and constraints of the several parties employing them, yet robust enough to maintain a common identity across sites. They are weakly structured in common use, and become strongly structured in individual-site use. They may be abstract or concrete. They have different meanings in different social worlds but their structure is common enough to more than one world to make them recognizable, a means of

translation. The creation and management of boundary objects is key in developing and maintaining coherence across intersecting social worlds.

So, for example, different participants from different social worlds may be brought together within organisations and yet have different commitments to versions of reality. They may espouse quite different and contradictory versions of the 'same thing' (the developing cells they call a fetus, the 'act' which happened in the grove of Rashomon, a televisually appropriate notion of follicular beauty, schizophrenia, sex or gender identity, what counts as a beard, and, as we shall see, many more 'realities'). So, in order to be able to cooperate, to 'share' a 'real world' of common objects and meanings, these participants create boundary objects that are, at least temporarily, compromises. The aim of these boundary objects is to satisfy 'these potentially conflicting sets of concerns' (Star and Griesemer, 1989: 413). Thus, boundary objects 'contain at every stage the traces of multiple viewpoints, translations and incomplete battles' (p. 413). These multiple viewpoints may be glossed over in actual situations of practice such that, in Garfinkel's terms, 'for all practical purposes' it may seem 'as if' everyone is focused on and talking about 'the same' thing.

Star and Griesemer suggest that this 'management' process is of great interest. It highlights how coherence, and thus the appearance of an ordered, 'real' and objective reality, are sustained across intersecting worlds and in ways that link these worlds together such that they seem to be shared (as long as the details of what is shared are not too deeply delved into). The concept of the boundary object lets us think about how an object's 'reality' flows or fluctuates across different ecological niches (within organisations, for example, but also geographical spaces) and how, in flux, objects are subject to different forms of understanding and enactment.

It is useful, now, to underline this point with a case study of how a seemingly 'real' object flows and comes to be differentiated as it moves from one ecological position to another. When we do we learn yet more about the nature of 'artful practices' and how they interact with the material world so as to make realities. Consider, then, the question of 'clean water'.

> ## CASE STUDY   Law and Mol on the bush pump and 'mutable immutable mobiles'
>
> John Law and Annemarie Mol (2001) describe how realities can be multiple and yet can be spoken of 'as if' their particular instances shared common characteristics, 'as if' the problem of multiple realities

were non-existent. Law and Mol develop this discussion through a case study of the Zimbabwe 'bush pump'. The bush pump, they describe, is composed of many parts. If the pump is to be deemed a 'good' technology, that is, worth implementing in policy terms, helpful and effective, then first and foremost, its components must work together so as to allow the pump actually to pump water, and, not only water, but water that is clean enough to drink.

While this point might initially seem trivial, as Law and Mol observe (and faintly echoing Cage on the Coca-Cola bottle), there is no one 'bush pump' *per se* - no two bush pumps are exactly alike. Rather, what counts as 'the pump' physically mutates from site to site as it is configured in different ways and according to what is needed and what is at hand (while the idea of the pump *qua* pump, a boundary object, implies that the pump is a stable and unvarying object). Thus, like George Washington's infamous axe (first the handle was replaced, then the blade, then the material that connected the two), Law and Mol observe that 'bits break off and are replaced with bits that don't seem to fit ... and other components ... are added to it ... which were not in the original design itself' (p. 614). And yet the pump is recognised as '*the* pump', from place to place; and, above any one place, it is hailed as a 'good' thing (for example, as an aid to public health). This mutable immutability extends, as Law and Mol describe it, even to the question of whether or not it is actually producing 'clean' water. As Law and Mol observe, 'the pump works if it produces clean water. But what counts as clean water? This, it turns out, is highly variable ...' (p. 614).

Configuring the pump's reality as effective means artfully putting it together so that it pumps 'clean' water. This 'putting together' is, however, *simultaneously* configuring our criteria of perception for the pump (What is clean-enough water? What is enough water?) and the actions, people and policies connected to this pump. The 'goodness' of the pump is thus a result of locally, contingently produced links between the pump's composition, criteria and technologies of assessment, and attribution. The pump - its mechanical form and the assessment of its value - is flexible; it 'mutates' over time and place. However, when the pump is discussed in abstract terms, these contingencies are effaced and replaced with a fixed identity.

The point is that goodness or effectiveness, in the case of the bush pump, is not self-evident. On the contrary, it is produced, time after time, from place to place, as both the bush pump and its value–identity are realised in relation to contextual factors that are *themselves* realised and selectively mobilised *as* contextualising factors. Context, in other words, is as much produced as producing. It is much more than a pre-existing set of constraints upon production or perception. As with the bush pump, so too for many other realities. The interaction between context and recognition is, in other words, produced, artfully, through the ways realities are linked to the material, linguistic and aesthetic features that give them their specific – and potentially contradictory – forms. Dirty water in time and place (a) may be clean in time and place (b). This is not 'mere' relativism; rather it is a recognition that realities take their defining shape in and through situated renditions, through, as we will now consider, the ways they are rendered or enacted and made manifest in local contexts.

Considering the question of mutable immutable mobiles helps us to see yet more clearly the point that realities are not made real through what people think, say or believe is real (though that comes into it), but rather, through artful practices that are often material practices, ones that join things together so as to make things seem 'useful, true, good and real'. (The term 'immutable mobile', referring to objects that can be carried from place to place and used to stabilise the meanings of things – a map, for example – is originally from Latour [1987].) I now want to develop the point about material cultural practice through two more examples – cookies in the first case, and disease, in particular atherosclerosis, in the second. The concepts introduced by these studies are, first, the notion of affordances and appropriations, and second, the idea that realities are not simply asserted (I say it is, you say it isn't) but enacted. Taken together, these matters serve to advance the notion that culture can never be determining, is never a simple backdrop, but is always a facilitating and constraining medium for achieving, to varying degrees and in varying configurations, our senses of reality as we flesh them out in practice.

CASE STUDY   Streeck on biscuits, or 'How to Do Things with Things'

As I have described elsewhere (DeNora, 2000: 38–41), in a 1996 piece entitled 'How to Do Things with Things', Streeck examines how a particular set of reality claims, namely that a brand of cookies is superior to its rival, is achieved through artful, material practice. Streeck describes a business meeting at a biscuit company where speakers – company executives – are tasting and talking about their product and their rival's product. To strengthen the arguments pro and con, the speakers do not merely speak about the biscuits, they let the biscuits, as it were, speak for themselves. By this I mean that the biscuits are drawn into communicative procedures that involve the artful arrangement of objects, the sensory properties of objects, utterances and valuations (of the cookies). So for example, because one brand of biscuit is crispy while another is chewy, action that seeks to 'reveal' the attributes of the crispy biscuit will, say, make resort to the biscuit's affordance of sound – when broken or bitten, the biscuit 'snaps' for example. The category 'good biscuit' is then defined in relation to snappiness (a texture but also a sound), rather than chewiness (a texture but not a sound). Thus 'reality' is not merely imposed from outside onto objects but involves working with objects to find ways of aligning them with, allowing their properties to instantiate, the categories they are seen to represent. (Conversely, one might suggest that a biscuit that snapped was 'too dry' and that 'biscuits should not be dry, like this one'.)

AFFORDANCES AND APPROPRIATIONS, AFFILIATIVE OBJECTS AND ATTACHMENTS

The point is that the biscuit (or anything else) has no one identity, no one reality status; rather it can lend itself – afford – different, and sometimes contradictory, identifications (crispy is good/bad). Its affordances, moreover, do not govern how it comes to be identified (e.g., a chair may become a table, a table a chair) but offer resources for use (DeNora, 2000: 40). Similarly, Anderson and Sharrock (1993) describe how objects' affordances are, as they put it, 'constituted and reconstituted in and through projected course of action within settings' (pp. 48–9).

Thus, objects do not offer, in any fixed sense, some pre-given set of affordances that can be described in advance of how objects come to be used. One cannot make definitive lists of what something means, what it might offer users, independent of use, because use (realignment, reappropriation) may profoundly transform what we discover about objects. So, for example, the biscuit's 'snap' is only discovered through the practices by which it is (a) broken or bitten so as to produce a sound and (b) linked to additional things, such as values that are in favour of or against the desirability of 'snappy'-sounding cookies.

Lucy Suchman clarifies this point in a study of, as she calls them, 'affiliative objects' (Suchman, 2005). Following Appadurai's (1986) notion of the social life of objects, and Gell's (1992: 43) focus on 'enchantments', Suchman describes how the identification of objects and people highlights a 'relational dynamics of association (and disassociation)'. Like the cookies described by Streeck, in other words, objects materialise social relations, realities. As such, Suchman's study points us ever more closely to a focus on objects and the ways that, by appropriating their affordances (which is simultaneously constituting the things that objects afford), we make and differentiate between realities. How objects, values and patterns of communicative action come to be clustered (artful practices) is how realities are rendered real – for a time, in a place, i.e., somewhere. So, a model of a photocopy machine, the Xerox 2800, was, within the context of Xerox PARC's research centre, affiliated with different objects and techniques that were linked to the varied interests and desires (subject positions) of personnel, including Suchman, at this site. Simultaneously, these objects drew out highly varied interests and subject positions as 'multiple possibilities that the object afforded us in living them' (2005: 394).

This point has been discussed in music sociology by Antoine Hennion (Gomart and Hennion, 1999; Hennion, 2007). Hennion describes how the 'attachments' people form to musical works or aspects of musical sound (a type of texture or sonority) constitute identity and of being together. One fixes on a given music and so finds a way of orienting to, of making, the world. This amateurism or, literally from the French, this love (of music), can become in other words a vital form of affiliative object for those who love, know how to love, and know how to preserve the love they feel for, music.

THE ARTFUL PRACTICES OF ENACTMENT

As we saw in the example of shyness and its recent pathologising, like actors, authors and others who play social roles, so too illnesses have 'careers'. Following the vicissitudes of those careers offers yet another methodological strategy for viewing realities as they are produced and tinkered with over time and space. In relation to medical realities, following those vicissitudes highlights the complex process by which categories of diagnosis, prognosis, aetiology, treatment and cure are configured and come to be established within medical classification schemes. It also highlights how these schemes are linked to institutional practices of health provision. These processes are of course interrelated with a host of mediating factors, and the history of medicine offers numerous cases where this shaping is contentious and – most interestingly – knowledge-based. In the 19th century, for example, puerperal insanity was the subject of rival knowledge claims between two groups, both with vested interests and both concerned to secure authority and economic dominion (Marland, 1999, 2004). On the one hand, midwives advocated keeping the patient at home and thus out of the grasp of the then-emerging specialists in 'mental alienation' (early psychiatry). On the other hand, mental alienists advocated relocating the mentally unwell to lunatic asylums and thus, under their own auspices.

In the 21st century, the factors that can mediate definitions of health and illness most often include techniques and technologies, research-funding priorities, lobby groups, policy cultures, systems of belief, discursive categories and iconic depictions in the media and the arts. Other factors include a widening raft of powerful players adjacent to the medical–industrial complex – HMOs (health maintenance organisations), pharmaceutical companies and insurers. In relation to these factors, the medical, paramedical and non-medical, the economic, the technical and the socio-cultural are often so mutually inflected that disentangling them becomes impossible. Moreover, in our time perhaps as never before, new categories of disease are emerging apace. This emergence is both symptom and cause of a medicalised culture in which increasing numbers of human conditions are pathologised (Conrad, 1987, 2007). But what *is* 'a' disease? How stable an object is disease even within the brief historical time frame of, say, one day? The answer is, not very, which, within the context of a hospital-based ethnography, led Annemarie Mol to speak of 'the body multiple'.

CASE STUDY   Mol on *The Body Multiple*

Annemarie Mol worked as an ethnographer in a Dutch hospital. She was interested in atherosclerosis, the accumulative obstruction of arteries. As the subtitle of the book describes, the study explores 'ontology in medical practice'. As a starting point, it is important to note that Mol's subtitle was not 'epistemology in medical practice' but rather, 'ontology', a concern with the nature of the disease itself. Knowledge, she argues, is not about reference (e.g., is this case an example of that category?) but of manipulation, and the question is not, as she puts it, 'how to find truth' but rather 'how are objects handled in practice?' (2002: 5). This question:

> does not concern the ways in which medicine knows its objects. Instead, what the book explores is the ways in which medicine attunes to, interacts with, and shapes its objects in its various and varied practices. Or, to use the technical term, this is a book about the way medicine *enacts* the objects of its concern and treatment. (2002: vii)

The focus on enactment takes Mol's study into what we have just explored as finitism, the notion that instances and categories of reality are produced simultaneously within contexts of use, through repeated, recursive, artful practices. In Mol's view, in other words, reality, even a physical reality such as the disease of atherosclerosis, is not merely 'there' as a

(Continued)

finished and unambiguous object that confronts perception and action, a category to which we simply match specific cases in the world. The question is not how we 'know' whether or not 'this' case is 'a' case of atherosclerosis but rather how we bring this case, and the category to which it belongs, to life in actual contexts of recognition, or as Mol terms it, enactment. The reality of disease takes shape, becomes manifest, through the ways it is approached, assessed and spoken about, through other things to which it is compared and to the tools that are used to measure and describe it. All of these connections have to be made by the actors who are doing the speaking and the looking at atherosclerosis and, as with the consideration of beauty in Chapter 6, those practices are artful.

Mol's contribution is to show how artful practices are both institutionally specific (e.g., as with Rosenhan and the diagnostic procedures employed in mental hospitals, so too with atherosclerosis there are hospital procedures that define the reality of the disease) and material/technical. The disease becomes a manifest reality, is enacted, in relation to the things that simultaneously describe or measure it and, through that seemingly 'neutral' practice, bring it into existence in spatially and temporally specific forms. How we come to look for, and recognise reality, and the materials, media, tools and words we use in this process, structures how realities lend themselves to our knowing.

Mol's focus is on the varied artful practices by which the object came to take on its identity or multiple identities as it passes from setting to setting, manipulation to manipulation, as its meanings were performed through verbal, material and representative practices, the practices moreover that are associated with the institutional processing of what we call atherosclerosis. This focus on the reality of the disease as it is constituted in and through contexts of use is finitist. Mol's focus moreover shifts the sociological lens from a focus on different perspectives or attitudes or beliefs about 'which' is the 'correct' reality (and thus a focus only upon the different 'views' that may be presented about what an object 'really is'), to a focus, as she says, on how realities are done. This focus relieves sociology from its otherwise highly constrained role as onlooker to quarrels and allows sociology to do something more profound – to examine how it is that such differences may come to seem compelling in, at times, quite contrary ways:

> This means ... talk about a series of different practices. These are practices in which some entity is being sliced, colored, probed, talked about, measured, counted, cut out, countered by walking, or prevented. Which entity? A slightly different one each time. Attending to enactment rather than knowledge has an important

effect: what we think of as a single object may appear to be more than one. All the examples in this book concern atherosclerosis. But a plaque cut out of an atherosclerotic artery is not the same entity as the problem a patient with atherosclerosis talks about in the consulting room, even though they are both called by the same name. The loss of blood pressure over a stenosis is not the same thing as the loss of blood vessel lumen that radiologists make visible on their X-ray pictures. (Mol, 2002: vii)

Mol describes how 'real objects' take shape through the ways that – in artful practice – they come to be linked to other things (policy, the built environment, procedures, concepts – e.g., 'cells', discourses and medical and scientific technologies). Practice, Mol argues, 'encompasses molecules and money, cells and worries, bodies, knives, and smiles, and talks about all of these in a single breath' (2002: 157).

This is 'hard' constructionism, i.e., not merely *labelling* a situation or condition but *producing* it through mediating procedures, materials and forms of perception that are linked to these practices. It is also 'super strong' cultural sociology. That is to say, and in keeping with the focus on the reflexive, performative practices that I described in Chapter 6 (where we saw the reality of beauty performed through the ways it was instantiated and coupled with many things that simultaneously configured both the category and the instances of beauty), Mol argues that diseases are 'enacted' through practice, multidimensional, lending themselves to multiple identities. The many versions of the disease 'atherosclerosis' are treated as if they adhere, as if they were all part of 'the same' thing within the hospital. Their differences, in other words, are reconciled and 'the' disease, despite its temporally and spatially varying format across the hospital's territories and times, is treated by all as if it were 'one' thing. In this attitude, one could argue, the idea and practices of treating atherosclerosis as 'a' disease is what holds the otherwise diverse parts of the institution together. Once again we see how the category (in this case a form of disease) modulates as it is enacted through different media, kaleidoscopically reconfiguring according to where and how it is positioned, in relation to what other things, by and for whom:

> If practices are foregrounded there is no longer a single passive object in the middle, waiting to be seen from the point of view of seemingly endless series of perspectives. Instead, objects come into being and disappear – with the practices in which they are manipulated. And since the object of manipulation tends to differ from one practice to another, reality multiples. The body, the

(Continued)

(Continued)

patient, the disease, the doctor, the technician, the technology: all of these are more than one. More than singular. This begs the question of how they are related. For even if objects differ from one practice to another, there are relations between these practices. Thus, far from necessarily falling into fragments, multiple objects tend to hang together somehow. Attending to the multiplicity of reality opens up the possibility of studying this remarkable achievement. (Mol, 2002: 5)

Just as disease is as a 'thing' itself multiple, so too there may be multiple views on the question of whether or not an individual 'has' an ailment and whether or not they are 'in need' of treatment. This issue will apply to many medical/healthcare realities – addiction, weight issues (overweight, eating disorders), responses to diagnoses (e.g., diet, exercise, meditation rather than medication for blood pressure) and various forms of (in Mol's terms) enactment that seek to transcend medicalised realities (e.g., refusing medical treatment for a life-threatening illness in favour of palliative care only, despite the likelihood of earlier death). They are perhaps most likely to be seen in cases involving mental health diagnoses, especially when associated with enforced hospitalisation.

Thus, it is one thing to describe how the reality of, in this case, a disease is multiple within the organisation, to follow, for example a 'case' of a disease as it moves, and undergoes translations, passages, as it is subject to varying defining technologies. Indeed, within many forms of organisations, 'the same' thing (a person, diagnosis, event, set of statistics) will take on different hues as it travels to different locations and is linked to yet different matters. Often these differences, which may be fundamental, can be glossed over and the concept of boundary object highlights how objects can mediate differences so that for all practical purposes they seem as if they are stable across time and location. But what happens when differences come to the fore, and rival enactments come into direct conflict? Here, the sociology of multiple realities merges with critical theory even if it does not take a stand. 'Which', to quote Humpty Dumpty, 'is to be Master?', a speaker or her words?

MULTIPLE REALITIES, CONTESTATION AND THE CULTURAL BASES OF 'POWER'

If realities are multiple, they are also contestable. And if they are contestable, then the upholding of one version of reality will have consequences for how participants relate to each other. We saw these consequences illustrated in Chapter 3 when we considered the example from Rosenhan's 'Being Sane in Insane Places'. What we did not explore then was how differential access to the means of defining realities and making them stick is achieved. It is time to consider that question explicitly, in terms of how access to the means of reality production are socially distributed and how that distribution in turn produces what sociologists speak of – in a short-hand way – as power differences. To explore this issue, consider how access to linguistic resources affects the ability of different participants in a situation to define that situation.

CASE STUDY   Mehan on reality disputes and the power of artful practices

Examining 'conflict talk', Mehan (1990) places passages of talk in a mental health hospital under the microscope. The talk (taken from the documentary film *Titicut Follies* [Wiseman, 1967]) occurred in the context of an assessment meeting; Mehan's focus is on particular passages of talk between a client (Vladimir) and a Head Psychiatrist who are disagreeing on a fundamental matter – the reality claim that Vladimir is not ill and that the mental hospital is making him ill, or not offering him resources with which to stay well. One of the passages that Mehan analyses goes like this:

Head Psychiatrist: Are you involved in any sports here?

Vladimir: There are no sports here. All I've got is a baseball and – and – a a glove, and that's it! There's nothing else. Hum. There's nothing else ...

Head Psychiatrist: Are you in any group therapy here?

Vladimir: No! There is no group, obviously I do not need group therapy. I need peace and quiet. See me. This place is disturbing me! It's harming me ... all I get is: 'Well, why don't you take medication?' Medication is disagreeable to me ...

Mehan examines how the Head Psychiatrist sets up a discursive format (illustrated in the excerpt of transcript above) in which Vladimir's conversational turns are restricted to yes/no responses. This discursive, local frame affords the psychiatrist's control of the conversation because it give him greater access to linguistic options or ways of talking. Establishing this conversational frame also sets up a paradox or

(Continued)

(Continued)

'Catch-22' situation: if Vladimir follows the rule he will be unable to engage as an equal in the verbal practice of situation definition; if, by contrast, he violates the rule in order to engage in that definition, he can be declared obstreperous.

Thus Mehan shows us how interaction can make use of background conditions and how this involves setting them up as 'appropriate' background conditions in the first place (in this case the categorical assumption that doctors 'must' have the right to ask the questions). This conditional set-up in turn conditions the ways in which each speaker may engage in resisting local practices of reality construction. Mehan concludes that the Thomas Theorem (with which we began Chapter 3), 'when men define situations as real they are real in their consequences' needs a slight revision as follows:

> All people define situations as real; but when powerful people define situations as real, then they are real for everybody involved in their consequences. (Mehan, 1990: 173)

At the same time Mehan offers an example whereby incommensurate versions of reality come into conflict, where the boundary objects of 'mental health' and 'treatment' are fraught and cannot simultaneously accommodate multiple notions of what they contain. Mehan describes how each of the speakers adheres to certain, opposing and incorrigible assumptions, and how this leads to a verbal impasse (it does not, however, lead to an impasse about Vladimir's further treatment – the doctor suggests that Vladimir is in need of further incarceration and a higher level of medication). To develop this point, Mehan turns to the anthropologist Evans Pritchard's study of the Azande and their practice of oracular reasoning to explain how commitment to an incorrigible proposition (I am not ill; he is ill) can 'frame' all subsequent interpretations, allowing for the 'same' pieces of information to serve as evidence for rival and indeed opposing claims. It is, in other words, nigh-impossible to 'see' a different definition of the situation because the parties to the dispute each adhere to reality claims in ways that cannot be confirmed or disconfirmed (1990: 173). As Mehan puts it:

> The doctors maintained the absoluteness of their belief in the patient's mental illness by denying, repelling, and transforming evidence which was contrary to their basic belief. The patient, too, used evidence presented in opposition to his argument as further support for the efficacy of his position. Thus, both a poorly educated, hospitalized patient and professionally educated physicians engaged in a similar reasoning process. They

admit to no universal standard (i.e., one that is outside both frames or in some frame acceptable by the people in the two frames) for judging the adequacy of ideas. As a result, no evidence or experience was allowed to count as disproof by either party. (1990: 173)

Thus, Mehan shows us how realities are asserted in ways that depend upon further assertions about the reality and identity of what is done within specific settings. But as Mehan describes, in this case the situation in which further assertions could be made was slanted; the linguistic playing field was not level. The incorrigible assumptions that prevailed were thus privileged by the situation, namely, those proposed by Vladimir's doctor. Mehan thus shows us how mere words, if they are not coupled to other empowering resources (such as enforced regulations of how participants may speak), are not enough. Key here, and a vital component of a cultural sociology of culture in action, is access to the means – verbal and material, social, practical – for the practical, artful crafting of cultural scenes and situations. How are these means distributed and how might access to them be differentially distributed, affecting opportunities for action, including opportunities for focus, deliberation and feeling secure about one's perceptions and beliefs? Consider situations where actors are separated from the means of cultural production, for example, in total institutions and under duress and recall Vladimir as discussed above, who had to make do with limited opportunities and means for expression.

CASE STUDY   Goffman on *Asylums*

The asylum's institutional practices and its built environment is intended to benefit inmates - to offer a place of healing and a place of security. Ironically, as Goffman describes, the removal of the inmate from access to routine cultural materials of expression - his or her own clothing, mundane objects and familiar furnishings - damages the inmate's sense of self because it removes the resources by which self is produced and reproduced. Inmates are, in other words, dispossessed of the means by which they would otherwise sustain themselves as selves. Within the asylum, the self is subject to mortification.

Goffman describes how inmates are in the paradoxical situation of having great need of, and minimal opportunity for, self-expression.

(Continued)

(Continued)

Given that resources for the self are scarce, inmates placed in totalising situations have great need but minimal opportunity for asylum seeking. They resort to whatever means are thus available, as Goffman describes in one of the most insightful passages ever written by a sociologist:

> [w]hen a patient, whose clothes are taken from him each night, fills his pockets with bits of string and rolled up paper, and when he fights to keep these possessions in spite of the consequent inconvenience to those who must regularly go through his pockets, he is usually seen as engaging in symptomatic behavior befitting a very sick patient, not as someone who is attempting to stand apart from the place accorded him. (1961: 307)

The very attempt to preserve oneself and to do so within a resource-impoverished setting, is read as evidence that this inmate requires further incarceration, that she or he is still unwell. That this observation is ironic is linked to the fact that these attempts to 'make do' are launched on an individual, and thus idiosyncratic, basis. If the patient who collects string were to collude with like-minded others, or if she/he were to gain attention and admiration for what she/he does from others, that patient would no longer appear quite so ill. But within the institutional setting, this form of collective action is prohibited, by force if necessary. Thus, Bennett Berger in his foreword to the 1986 edition of Goffman's *Frame Analysis* (written shortly after Goffman's death), suggested that because of Goffman's:

> analytical focus on the most minute details of interaction, Goffman often seemed to exclude from consideration the impact of forces and variables beyond the frame of the situation at hand, and therefore seemed to suggest, as many symbolic interactionists did, that the situation could be fully understood as a self-contained unit of analysis without recourse to matters outside its frame.

But behind all this apparently symbolic interactionist focus there was another (perhaps gloomier) Goffman, a scholar strongly influenced by the macrosociological tradition of Emile Durkheim, which he absorbed through the functionalism of British social anthropology. Goffman of course did not give much close attention to the study of major social institutions (the mental hospital was about as close as he got) but he surely knew that behind all the face-to-face goings on that did claim his research attention there were large, sturdy, and durable institutional structures that distributed the resources of interaction (power, prestige, social skills, for example) unequally ... (in Goffman, 1986: xv–xvi)

To an extent, Berger may be overplaying (and under-theorising) organisational structures, taking their power and hierarchical practices as a given rather than exploring the situated and artful practices by which an organisation's structure is hypothetically always subject to challenge and continually renewed through situated, artful practice. And yet Berger was right to highlight, as he put it, the ways in which 'the resources of interaction' are socially distributed and typically not in egalitarian ways.

In short, as we have seen in the different examples presented in this chapter, realities may be multiple but that multiplicity is often narrowed through the ways that spaces for action are furnished and through the ways that *access* to those furnishings is distributed. To define situations as real requires, as we have so far seen, much more than mere words, though words, and access to forms of words, may well be a useful medium of situation definition. Situations are defined, realities enacted, through the artful practices by which perception, action and interpretation are steered in certain ways, through control over the resources for making sense of things. These practices involve engaging with materials, controlling access to materials and instantiating general categories. Realities are crafted, not simply described or asserted, and that crafting takes shape in the spaces between individuals. It is neither micro nor macro. That is to say, that just as individuals, or even some individuals, cannot 'steer' interaction at will, so too, interactions are not predetermined by formal structures – organisational hierarchies for example. Rather, sociological variables such as power and status, and more fundamentally ontological matters such as identities, definitions of situations, and the meaning of physical things, take shape in and through the artful practices by which actors connect the proximate, or the here and now of specific instances (interactions, individuals, situations) with the distal or the then and there of types of things, forms, codes, rules and categories.

The key point here is that this artful practice itself takes shape according to which resources for enacting realities are accessible. If realities are enacted by appropriating resources that afford certain meanings and representations, that enactment is itself structured by the ways that affordances for meaning-making are distributed within the site of ongoing interaction. To adopt this position is to eschew both micro and macro sociology and to understand them as presenting a false dichotomy, one that is not set up to investigate properly and fully the ways in which specific instances (of people, things, physical matter) come to be aligned with, but also instantiate, more general categories of what those things could mean. And both the micro and the macro perspectives, with their respective emphases on structures and individual actors, offer blunt instruments for the precise dissection of just how realities are enacted, and enacted with consequences for who and what can be. How is it, then, that we so often genuinely believe in particular versions of reality, actually seeing them as tangible and unambiguous and, thus, as matters of fact and things we 'must' accept? It is now time to consider the question of where and how structures of perception are themselves constructed and how this is a vital topic for cultural sociology. Or, to put this as Goffman does, quoting William James (1950), '*under what circumstances do we think things are real?*' (Goffman, 1986 [1977]: 2, emphasis in original). It is now time to look yet more closely at how and under what conditions, as Goffman says, our senses of reality come to be generated and make themselves available to perception. That process involves, I suggest, an understanding of practical magic.

PART 3

ARTFUL PRACTICES AND MAKING SENSE

8

MAKING SENSE OF REALITY: PERCEPTION AS ACTION

To speak about realities – multiple, contrary – as they are enacted is, perhaps inevitably, to speak about the links between perception, culture and practice in real-time social situations. Indeed, perception is reconfigured within this perspective as yet another form of practice – the production of *attention* – linked to and mutually determining of culture. As Mack and Rock, the authors of *Inattentional Blindness*, put it (recall this concept was discussed in Chapter 1 via the 'gorilla' study of Simons and Chabris, 1999), 'there seems to be *no conscious perception without attention*' (Mack and Rock, 1998: ix, emphasis in original).

Mack and Rock suggest that conscious perception arises from meaningful framing such that the swirling, and potentially multiply-meaningful, *mess* of stimuli come to be recognised in particularly meaningful ways. Citing William James' comment (1981: 395) about how 'a faint tap per se' may escape attention while a faint tap interpreted as the possible signal of a lover tapping quietly on a window pane will capture attention, they conclude that, 'nothing is seen without attention' (Mack and Rock, 1998: 229) and that 'simple, low-level features of stimuli are perceived preattentively and therefore provide the basis for the capture of attention that is essential to the construction of objects from preattentively perceived features' (p. 229).

Once again, Mary Douglas offers an excellent point of departure for the cultural sociology of attentive perception:

Perceiving is not a matter of passively allowing an organ – say of sight or hearing – to receive a ready-made impression from without, like a palette receiving a spot of paint. Recognising and remembering are not matters of stirring up old images of past impressions. It is generally agreed that all our impressions are schematically determined from the start. (Douglas, 2002 [1966]: 37)

Douglas is saying that perception is encultured, that it is selective and characterised by a human predisposition to look for patterns. She suggests that perception organises shifting sensory impressions into 'recognisable shapes' and that 'in perceiving we are building' in ways that dispense with features that seem to contradict preconceived patterns:

> As time goes on and experiences pile up, we make a greater and greater investment in our system of labels. So a conservative bias is built in. It gives us confidence … (Douglas, 2002 [1966]: 37)

To be sure, and despite her insightful commentary, Douglas' vision is not perfect. Her 'conservative bias' offers what might be considered to be an idealised model of how perception occurs, as if cultural prescriptions, once learned, allow viewers to 'see' the patterns that culture offers. And yet we have already seen how ways of seeing are multiple, varied and often inconclusive. What is perhaps of greater interest, and more powerful as a mode of explaining how culture 'gets into' action, is to examine the practices by which we perceive in the zero-hour of everyday life, in real-time situations. Such a focus, moreover, helps us better to understand the problem of multiple realities, or why it is that our perceived worlds may be incommensurate: there is, as we will now begin to explore, not only more to notice than can be noticed (Douglas' 'chaos'), there are also many ways that perception can be linked to categories and thus enacted as reality. These linkages – and the anchoring devices that stabilise them – require airing. How, then, do we 'fit' categories of reality with what we encounter moment to moment as the swirling, often ambiguous phenomena of our daily experience encountered in the moment? How does perception become attention and identification, and how then does identification become enactment, and how does all of this occur *in situ*? And, moving on from Douglas to embrace the reflexivity that I described in Chapter 6, how might we regard all action, all perception as *simultaneously* culturally produced and cultural production? To examine this set of questions I will begin with an example from Wittgenstein.

Figure 8.1   Wittgenstein's doodle revealed as a duck

First published in Wittgenstein, Ludwig (2009) *Philosophische Untersuchungen/ Philosophical Investigations*. Revised fourth edition. Oxford: Wiley-Blackwell. Reprinted with kind permission from Wiley.

WHICH REALITY? WITTGENSTEIN ON 'SEEING'

As Wittgenstein puts it:

> Should I say: 'The picture-rabbit and the picture-duck look just the same'?! Something militates against that – But can't I say: they look just the same, namely like this – and now I produce the ambiguous drawing. (The draft of water, the draft of a treaty.) But if I now wanted to offer reasons against this way of putting things – what would I have to say? That one sees the picture differently each time, if it is now a duck and now a rabbit – or, that what is the beak in the duck is the ears in the rabbit, etc.? (1980: 16)

To begin with, let's say that the drawing (Figure 8.1) is of a duck. More specifically, if we see this diagram as a drawing of a duck it is because we actively focus upon certain aspects of what is on the page (the duck's eye, beak, perhaps the duck-like rounded head) and draw them into relation with a pre-existing, already known-to-us concept, namely, duck. Materially, we hold the drawing (or the angle of our head) so that the duck is 'right side up'. Simultaneously, we may actively suppress details that might contradict our visual commitment to the idea that this is a duck (the slight indentation on the back of the duck's head). If we do notice an aberrant detail, and remain or wish to remain committed to the idea that the drawing is a duck, then we probably also find ways of accounting for this discrepancy from 'duckness'. For example, we might define the indentation as accidental or incidental. We might say, 'Oh, well, there is where Wittgenstein's hand slipped as he was drawing the animal' or 'Perhaps there is a duck with ruffled feathers or an unusual shaped head, or which was once in an accident and thus has a slight dent in the back of his head'.

When we do these things we are engaging in what I have already described as the artful practice of reality enactment. In relation to the perception of Wittgenstein's doodle as a duck, this artful practice involves our 'bearing with' a reality claim even when, perhaps, we have our doubts, or cannot quite 'see' the instance as the category. It involves our tacit dismissal of 'aberrant' details that might contradict the drawing's 'duckness' (such as the dent in the duck's head). Similarly, it includes how we will 'make do' with imperfect versions of what we take to be an underlying form or identity (in this case duck-ness). And, it involves the adding-in of extras, 'filling in' aspects of forms that might not actually be present in a particular instance of the form as we encounter it (e.g., I 'see' the duck's feathers even when they are not actually drawn in this diagram; I transpose from one duck to another).

So, for example, looking at the drawing and adhering to the proposition that we are encountering a drawing of 'a duck', we complete the duck drawing (enact it *as* a drawing of a duck) by providing missing features, projecting them on or into the instance at hand (feathers, a quack, the rest of the duck's body, the iridescent feathers around its neck) and fending off rival realities (see below). Through these practices we establish the 'for all practical purposes' reality that the lines upon the paper depict a duck. We then orient to this instance (of a duck) 'as if' it was already that which we made it into. Our perception was in other words an active part of this seemingly passive perception of this drawing (of a duck).

There are, accordingly, many tasks to be accomplished before the duck becomes, to the eye of the beholder, a duck, a 'given' and unproblematic reality for 'anyone' to behold. Or as Wittgenstein puts it:

> When we look at the figure, our eyes scan it repeatedly, always following a particular path. The path corresponds to a particular pattern of oscillation of the eyeballs in the act of looking. It is possible to jump from one such pattern to another and for the two to alternate.... Certain patterns of movement are physiologically impossible; hence, for example, I cannot see the schematic cube as two interpenetrating prisms. And so on. (1958: 212e)

Wittgenstein points to the active searching that we do with our eyes – and without any conscious awareness of the practice ('pattern of oscillation of the eyeballs in the act of looking'). Looking, in other words, is active, constitutive. In recent years, research in the area of eye tracking has served to document our 'ways of looking' so to speak.

GAZE TRACKS

Eye tracking is an area of research that uses infra-red capture devices to monitor the direction, frequency and duration of visual focus on objects (animate, inanimate), art works, technologies (such as computer screens or flight control consoles) and physical settings (such as supermarket shelving). So for example, it is possible to document such matters as 'the first look, longest look, total looking time and number of fixations as well as clustering of the fixations for identifying regions of interest which were subsequently plotted on top of the pictures' (Kovic et al., 2009: 421). So too, researchers can track the detail of where we look when attempting to make sense of visual objects. The method is increasingly used to evaluate website navigability (Duchowski, 2007; Katsanos et al., 2010).

So, for example, Holmqvist et al. (2011) have described how looking at Leonardo Da Vinci's famous painting, the *Mona Lisa*, involves a temporal sequence of foci: the eye moves over time, lingering longer and less long on different features of the painting (longer on the mouth for example). Some features of the painting are (literally) hotter than others (e.g., the face, the hands) because this is where the infra-red capture of eye focus shows greatest time being spent. The eye-tracking method shows us how seeing – or seeing understood as perception – involves selective accumulation as a visual stimulus is processed.

Here we can begin to appreciate the ways in which perception involves the use of culture – framing – in action. Eye tracking highlights how viewing or perceiving visual stimuli – or at least some visual stimuli – both occurs in patterned ways *and adds* pattern to what we behold. It also shows us, graphically, how different individuals look in similar ways: what they look at and what they do not look at. The idea that we are all looking at the same thing when we look at something is, of course, simplistic, but eye tracking shows us that the thing we take to be the object is in fact an object-multiple. What then is responsible for perceptual order and thus for a shared perceptual world? Here we need to consider the ways in which perception is social activity, how it takes shape in relation to things outside the eye and brain of the individual recipient, and thus how it can be structured in ways that may result in seeing, and not seeing, things in particular ways.

So far, I have described how we do not simply 'see' the figure of a duck. Rather we organise our perceptual processing *in accordance with* some presumptions and expectations (theoretical propositions in other words) of what we are likely to, expect to, find. These ideas have been a part of image processing theory in computer graphics since its inception (Tudhope and Oldfield, 1982). Thus, if you say to me, 'Look at this bad picture of a duck', you are also inviting, instructing, perhaps, under some circumstances, even commanding me about *how* to look. At that stage, assuming I am already familiar with the bird 'duck' and, in memory of Durkheim on French, that I understand/have learned the English term (you do not say 'canard' [French] or 'pato' [Portuguese]), I will look selectively, searching for the relevant features – the beak, eye, rounded head, neck shape.

Labels thus are contextualisation cues (see DeNora, 1986); as such they are also instructions for, invitations to, a form of reality. If I say 'this is a duck', I am inviting you to 'see' the drawing 'as if' it were a duck. That invitation is a tacit invocation to the senses to engage in a particular form of artful practice: 'Organise search procedures in *this* way, not *that* way! Look here, not there!' We make these sorts of invocations, often, perhaps especially in the context of domestic and intimate cultures, or craft-based cultures, when we seek to instruct each other about how to

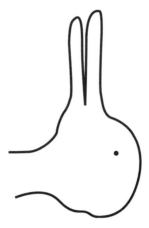

Figure 8.2 Wittgenstein's doodle revealed as a rabbit

First published in Wittgenstein, Ludwig (2009) *Philosophische Untersuchungen/ Philosophical Investigations.* Revised fourth edition. Oxford: Wiley-Blackwell. Reprinted with kind permission from Wiley.

sense ('Take a bit of this and then taste the wine again'; 'Hold the bow at this slightly different angle and this pressure and notice how the sound is different'). But on many occasions in everyday life we give this level of detailed engagement a miss, in part because it takes time, it is slow (so we simply say to each other, 'nice wine' and use that as a proxy for more detailed calibrations of perceptive faculties).

So, perception itself can iron out ambiguity ('ah, yes, now I see that it is a duck'); it can deflect the possibility of contradictory realities ('and of course it could not be anything but a duck'); or, alternately, it can enhance them ('look at that dent on the back of its head: that could not be a duck! Indeed, you need to turn the picture sideways. *It's a rabbit* not a duck!') (see Figure 8.2). For all of these things, it is not sufficient to merely look 'more closely' (as if under a magnifying glass, quantitatively). The recognition of a meaningful object requires qualitative forms of looking (angles, handling, preparation, search procedures), and that involves more artful practice – namely processes and techniques that can organise perception and thus increase the possibility that it can be shared.

ILLUSION INVOLVES COLLUSION

I have been suggesting that the 'work' (or ethnomethods) that we do as actors to stabilise our world and its realities includes our habits and practices of perception. The structuration of perception – dear to the heart of politicians, rhetoricians and advertisers (and beautifully considered by Goffman in his *Frame Analysis* [1986]) – is thus also a vital aspect of what we need to examine if we are to understand how realities are made, buttressed and undercut in everyday life. By calling perception to order with different instructions we may find perception's object takes very different forms, and here we have yet another reason why multiple realities and conflicts over the nature of reality in everyday life come about. Where we look, coupled with assumptions about how to look (what might be found, what would I expect to be important features, what is noise), produce what we take to be 'really' there, what is important versus insignificant and therefore 'safely' ignored. This process of perception is historically important because it conditions perception the next time round: how, then, is what we saw the last time we looked consequential for what we see the next time we look? Consider an example from Agatha Christie.

CASE STUDY   Agatha Christie's *Evil Under the Sun*

In Agatha Christie's novel set on Burgh Island in south Devon, the detective Hercule Poirot accompanies the Chief Constable, Colonel Weston, to the scene of the crime, a beach surrounded by cliffs, accessed by a long ladder from the cliff top to the beach. By the ladder, a collection has been made of objects found, understood as potential 'clues':

> A small collection of objects was laid out neatly on a rock. There was a pair of scissors, an empty gold flake packet, five patent bottle tops, a number of used matches, three pieces of string, one or two fragments of newspaper, a fragment of a smashed pipe, four buttons, the drumstick bone of a chicken and an empty bottle of sun-bathing oil. (Christie, 2001 [1941]: 214)

The narrator then describes how Weston considered the various objects. The scissors he notes are 'bright and shining' and thus not left out in the rain of the day before. They were found, along with the fragment of a pipe, at the base of the ladder. In consultation with the police officer on duty and Hercule Poirot, an implicit decision about the relative importance of these clues is made: the scissors are described as 'ordinary' and the pipe as good quality, to which Poirot comments that one of the suspects said he had 'mislaid' his pipe (p. 214).

Here in Christie's account, one that is of course deliberately designed to tease the reader, objects are implicitly arranged in terms of potential significance. The buttons are ignored, the bottle explained away ('been here some time'). The scissors, which have apparently not been on the beach for some time (or else they would be rusted) receive no further comment while a fragment of a pipe, apparently an expensive one, is found and subsequently discussed by the characters over several paragraphs. It is noted that *the husband of the victim smokes a pipe*. In real time, or rather in the book's and reader's time, invitations to possible, and contradictory, meanings are issued; invocations about looking, where to look, what is important or a salient feature are also issued and in ways that direct the search for meaning and pattern. So, for example, in the excerpt quoted above, the search turns to those potential suspects who smoke pipes. One can map the flows of attention and, with these flows, the avenues by which potential clues and rival interpretations (albeit temporarily in the case of this whodunnit) come to be lost (see Figure 8.3).

Without spoiling the plot, it is possible to say that the process runs as follows: the focus on the pipe directs attention to the characters who are pipe smokers and to whether any of them have misplaced their pipes. Associated with this flow of attention is the question of whether the pipe smokers have alibis. If not, then attention can flow again to the question of motive. Meanwhile, attention is deflected from the scissors and the buttons, and the trail that might, or might not, lead from them grows cold. In sum we see how culture (in this case assumptions about what is important) can provide prescriptions for viewing what there is to see, filtering some things out, placing some

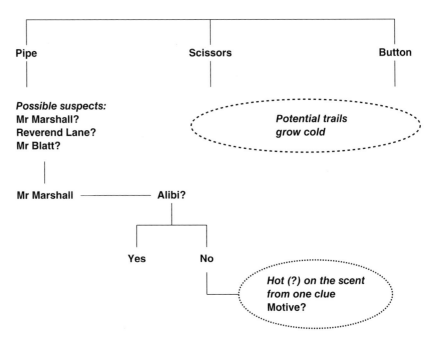

Figure 8.3 Seeing and not seeing significance at the scene of the crime in Agatha Christie's *Evil Under the Sun*

things in the foreground and others in the background. As time passes, it may become difficult, if not impossible, to 'see it all three ways' as one might have done earlier on. This is due in part to the fact that habits of thought/perception congeal through repetition; they develop, as it were, careers within the constructed account of what happened and what there might be to know more about. The careers of these perceptual habits are further extended through talk and action ('We have all agreed that the only thing of interest here is the pipe' or 'This is a half-decent drawing of a duck but a bad drawing of a rabbit'). But they also become extended as links between them and institutional and material practices such as technologies of detection and methods of police work. So, for example, the object-clues are especially important because this Agatha Christie murder, which takes place on a beach, is devoid of weapons, footprints and fingerprints. Moreover, because the story is set (and the novel written) in 1941, as opposed to 2014, there is no DNA evidence.

MAGIC AND MISDIRECTION

Agatha Christie not only uses but also writes, compellingly, about the procedures that make conjuring tricks so successful (see Latour [1988] on the specific tactic of shifting out and in, spatially, actorially and temporally within a narrative). Indeed, one might argue, she writes as well and knowingly on this topic as any sceptical philosopher of scientific knowledge. In *They Do It With Mirrors* (Christie, 1993 [1952]) Christie makes these points explicit and uses the whodunnit as a vehicle for discoursing eloquently on the matter of illusion and reality. We see a part of something that we assume is a greater whole and we infer – or take a theoretical shortcut – to that whole, presuming that it 'must' be there. We dwell upon those things that confirm this hypothesis and we deflect contradictory evidence. As we do this, and as with *Evil Under the Sun*, an alternative set of 'scents' grows cold.

CASE STUDY   Agatha Christie's *They Do It With Mirrors*

'No,' said Miss Marple. 'It's not a question of what people have said. It's really a question of conjuring tricks. They do it with mirrors, you know - that sort of thing - if you understand me.' (Christie, 1993 [1952]: 201)

(Continued)

At this point the inspector to whom Miss Marple has just spoken wonders if Miss Marple is in possession of all her mental faculties. Miss Marple goes on to explain that he needs to consider the room they are standing in as if it were a stage set; the inspector must imagine that he were in the audience watching the action unfold, in particular the entrances and exits of the various characters. She points out that, from the audience, we rarely consider where the characters go to when they exit. She concludes:

'But really of course they go out to the wings - or the back of the stage with carpenters and electricians, and other characters waiting to come on - they go out - to a different world.' (Christie, 1993 [1952]: 205-6)

Miss Marple describes how the conjurer is able to structure our perception so that we 'see' what we believe to be there. Our perception is directed to some things and deflected from others. So too a conjurer who performs a trick – take the example of the vanishing coin (Figure 8.4) – deceives by playing upon the ways in which attention can never be everywhere simultaneously but rather selectively focuses upon some features of an event, object or encounter. This selective attention is structured by the magician, in much the same way that our attention can be structured in ways that enable us to perceive Wittgenstein's doodle as a duck, or rabbit. The magician exploits two things in tandem. First, she/he exploits our expectancies (e.g., if you are holding a coin in your hand I would see it; if you are holding a coin in your hand and put your hand palm down, the coin would fall to the ground). Second, she/he exploits our habit of focusing on what, in real time, seems like 'important' information (you are waving your right hand around and my eyes are trained on that active hand; meanwhile I pay no attention to what your left hand is 'doing' because it seems to me that there is nothing there to see).

In the case of the coin trick and in the case of how the murder was done in *They Do It With Mirrors*, the 'audience' interprets events that are conditioned by highly crafted, structured displays of information. This structuring is designed to lead the audience to reach conclusions about what they see/what happened based on highly mediated, pre-theorised data. This selective attention exemplifies yet again the concept (introduced in Chapter 1) of 'inattentional blindness' (Mack and Rock, 1998; Simons and Chabris, 1999), more specifically, the ways in which inattentional blindness can be directed, and that topic highlights in turn the

Palming – both hands seem to be empty.

The 'backstage' – the coin 'held' in the palm of the hand.

Figure 8.4 The vanishing coin trick: hand positions

extent to which procedures of perception are or can be shared. In the case of the coin trick, one holds the coin in a slightly curved hand (the technique is known as 'palming'). Caught in the fleshy part of the palm of a very slightly cupped hand, the coin is secure even when the hand is turned upside down or waved about 'as if' it were empty. Meanwhile, we, the audience, are not (or were not) conscious of how the hand can hold in this way – we assume the hand could not hold the coin because it is displayed palm downward. As the palm turns downward, the hand converts itself *through its action and in conjunction with prior assumptions about how things work* into something that – without much conscious effort – we interpret as something 'not worth watching': after all, we might say, the palm is facing down, therefore the hand 'must' be empty (recall the dangers associated with the word 'must' which I discussed in Chapter 1). This allocation of attention (what to pay attention to, what not; foreground and background) completes the set of ingredients required for a successful conjuring trick: reception is as important as display in other words. Thus the trick 'does its magic'.

There are, of course, many forms of display that direct and/or seek to direct perceptual activity, to encourage the eye – or ear, nose, hand or tongue – to sense in particular ways. To put this point slightly differently, misdirection involves exploiting learned and typically unconscious perceptual procedures by setting up circumstances in which these procedures will be, most likely, used. As with being able to 'see' the duck (or rabbit) in Wittgenstein's doodle, so too (if the trick succeeds, if the duck is found) the viewer's perception is harnessed (the viewer herself colludes in this process, allowing her perception to be harnessed or attuned to specific focal points and cues) in ways that lead to noticing precisely what is (the duck) or is not (the coin) relevant.

In the words of the magician known as Teller, magic is, 'the theatrical linking of a cause with an effect that has no basis in physical reality, but that – in our hearts – ought to' (Macknik and Martinez-Conde, 2011: 194).

This summary is, I think, not quite right because it depicts magic's effects as having 'no basis in physical reality' (i.e., its effects are merely illusory, as if magic were 'unreal' and reality were 'real'). If we accept this dichotomy – illusion versus reality – then to speak of reality's production as akin to magic (arising from artful practices) implies that reality is all in the mind's eye, illusory. But there is a subtle difference between the words 'artful' (skilful, crafted, creative) and 'artificial' (contrived, fake, substitute for). The presented reality of magic (e.g.; a woman sawn in half, a disappearing coin) is illusory but, as Miss Marple remarked, the activity of magic (what it does with that woman, that coin) is not illusory. To the contrary it is as real as anything else we might wish to consider. This is to say that magic *does* have a basis in physical reality – it is dependent upon the cup-like shape that a hand can make, on the physical practices of looking and on movement/gesture in time. In this respect, magic is just one more form of artful practice, one that in this case is devoted to the business of deceit or rather to the induction of perception (and its byproduct, the production of deception) through carefully drawing together meanings, physical procedures, materials and movements in time. It was this that Agatha Christie wanted to teach us in *They Do It With Mirrors* when she presents a conversation between the Inspector and another character in which they conclude that 'a stage set's real enough', that is, made from actual materials and is equally real 'behind the scenes as it is in front' (Christie, 1993 [1952]: 181).

FORMS OF PERCEPTION

In passing, a brief word about my focus, so far, upon the visual. I have been focused on the sense of sight, but similar points could be made using other sensory modalities – hearing, smell, taste, touch. Indeed, the senses as realities are themselves subject to reassessment in terms of their mutual reliance on cultural set-ups to the extent that there may be no distinction in practice between prosthetic and 'natural' ways of sensing (Hara and DeNora, 2013). So too they are mutually constituting, for example, when one sense is used as a proxy or in a supportive way to enhance or substitute for another: we may 'see' with our sense of touch and 'touch' with our sense of sight (see Chapter 9 on how the 'blind' can be said to 'see' what is not available to the eyes). So too, different senses may be privileged in different social contexts at the larger collective level; for example, for the Kaluli of Papua New Guinea, sound is the primary sensory modality for navigation in dense rainforest settings (Feld, 2012). Similarly, within the confines of the medical consultation, or in preparation/consumption, or in intimate encounters, smell, touch and taste may be more important, at least sometimes, than sight. In recent years, as Pink (2004) explains, there has been a shift in how people's sensory worlds are treated by researchers:

> Although in general anthropologists (perhaps especially visual anthropologists) have attended insufficiently to the senses other than the visual … key works … demonstrate the importance of seeking out how non-visual sensory experience, understanding and knowledge are relevant in particular contexts … (Pink, 2004: 145)

The set-ups that facilitate particular forms of perception can be understood to enhance and extend perception and to structure it, to render it fit for certain purposes, less fit for others. In this sense, one could argue, the perception of reality is always a virtual and prosthetic form of perception, one that is mediated and takes shape in relation to technologies that enable and configure perception in the first place. By this logic, there is no 'natural' form of perception, but rather there are different modalities that sensory capacity can assume. For example, it is possible to 'hear' through the sense of touch, to 'see' through the sense of sound, to 'feel' through the sense of sight, as in the next example which addresses our sense of proprioception – our experience of our bodies and bodily sensation – and how this sense is itself organised through the socio-technical and cultural crafting of situations and frames for perception. Consider the famous 'rubber hand' illusion.

CASE STUDY   Enacting sensation and the rubber hand illusion

The rubber hand illusion refers to a series of experiments that produced phantom sensation and a misattribution of embodiment. Research subjects were positioned such that one of their hands was hidden by a drape, while a rubber hand was positioned both in sight and in such a way that it gave the appearance of being the subject's own hand (the rubber hand was positioned in parallel to the subject's other hand on a table). Both hands - the subject's real hand and the rubber hand - were then stroked and tapped in an identical and synchronised manner while subjects were instructed to look at the fake hand. Subjects reported the sense of believing that the fake hand was actually their real hand.

The rubber hand illusion illustrates how one sense modality (visual information) can be used to 'capture' (Legrand, 2007: 695) another (tactile information) in ways that significantly alter aspects

(Continued)

(Continued)

of self-consciousness and orientation. As such it also highlights the interconnection between the senses of sight and touch and the production of proprioception (the sense of one's body position). Here, then, the circumstances of sensory information processing are thus capable of 'tricking' the brain, or rather, tricking the ways that subjects' brains processed sensory stimulation/information. Key here, as an introduction to music and pain management, is that the rubber hand experiment highlights how matters external to the embodied and perceiving subject can structure the ways that this subject perceives seemingly internal sensations.

The rubber hand illusion serves to highlight how, within the human and medical sciences, we need make no distinction between 'cultural' realities and 'natural' or physical ones since they are better understood to be mutually constitutive. The case of pain management serves to illustrate this point. It shows us how perception does not occur 'in' or 'by' individuals alone but rather emerges *in relation to* culturally learned and culturally mobilised forms of apparatus or set-ups that, to varying extents, structure the typically tacit, pre-conscious anticipation of 'what there is to see' and thus 'what is seen' (or felt or heard or smelled). Proprioception is, in other words, socio-culturally produced. So, sensing can be mediated through anticipation, and anticipation itself mediated through cultural forms. The power of framing and suggestion, then, can create sensory illusion, which is real in its consequences.

The rubber hand illusion opens a rich seam for the sociology of realities. First, it shows us how even as seemingly private a matter as embodied awareness takes shape in relation to things outside of individuals. Second, it takes us well beyond (to use the old terminology) the social construction of reality and into, as Mol terms it, the *enactment* of realities. This enactment involves much more than social practices; it involves, as we have seen, interactions with, appropriations of and representations through materials and technologies. The question then, of when, how and if sensory illusions can become sensory realities, is potentially of immense importance to a range of research areas, perhaps most especially for the field of health humanities. It speaks to the topic of placebos (increasingly receiving attention in medical research) and the related field of pain management, both areas once thought to be immured from 'soft' subjects in the social sciences, arts and humanities. Even if such illusions provide only temporary respite from pain or anguish, the respite or 'room' (to retain the 'asylum' analogy) that is achieved may provide resources for further repair work - blood flowing back into muscles, or the kick-start of a virtuous circle of mental depression such as getting out of the house again after a period of isolation, to take examples from both the 'physical' and 'mental' health realms. The potential lines of investigation into this mind/body/culture area are numerous and the surface has only been scratched.

These areas require new questions. For example, how might individuals be trained or come, informally, to learn how to 'trick' their perception in ways that translate sensation? How might these 'tricks' be linked to cultural set-ups, by which I mean arrangements of materials and practices (objects and their positionings, gestures, verbal cues, handlings of objects, pairing with claims about situations and their definitions and physical/social locations [what can happen or be perceived in a church, in a mental hospital, in a kitchen]) so as to prioritise particular perceptual outcomes? And how can such 'tricks' be managed so that they can be pursued without endangering the patient/client? (For example, under some circumstances feeling 'pain free' is not a good thing; indeed it can be life threatening). Here, neuroscientific accounts of how the anticipatory and sympathetic mirror responses work can benefit from dialogue with health–music studies and from current working knowledge in music therapy. In earlier work (DeNora, 2013) I describe these issues and how they raise important questions about the reality of embodied sensation.

CASE STUDY   DeNora on musicking the pain away

In recent years sociological studies of the corporeal have shifted from a focus on 'the' body to a focus on forms of embodiment, a way of acknowledging that there is no one human body but rather bodies multiple, bodies that are enacted - in Mol's terms - in relation to and through practices, materials and meanings. But what of seemingly 'real', physical matters, such as pain? Is pain itself the product of enactment and can pain be modified through artful practice? If so, then it is possible to speak of reality construction at the deepest level, one at which nature and culture are mutually determining.

To put this slightly differently, if embodied phenomena - sensation, proprioception - vary according to cultural set-ups, then embodied phenomena involve more than physiology, more than brain, and more than mind/body interaction. That 'more' is the social, technical and aesthetic apparatus and an ecological conception of consciousness (primary and secondary). We have thus returned to the place where practical experience (I respond sympathetically because I have 'been there and done that and experienced this'), framing and informal social learning through

(Continued)

(Continued)

interaction with others, and modelling of how others do or experience things, coalesce. This is also the place to recall the lessons from Howard Becker (discussed in Chapter 4) on the mutual determination of sensation, perception, learning, disposition, framing and milieu over time. Of additional interest is whether neural activity can be seen as the mechanism responsible for music's effects, or whether it is the byproduct of socio-cultural orientation. How much, in other words, need we concern ourselves with neuroscience to understand and use music as a health technology and health-humanities media? To develop this theme it is useful to consider the realm of music and pain management.

The focus on the importance of apparatus helps to explain music's effectiveness as a medium of pain management and also helps revitalise the long history of music's role in healing (Gouk, 2000; Horden, 2000). In particular, it highlights pain as a complex experience rather than a universal neurobiological condition; in other words, as involving more than reports to the brain's pain centre. By contrast, pain is now more often conceptualised as a cultural, emotional, personal and situated matter (Hanser, 2010: 857) in which the same stimuli may be met with very different responses by different individuals.

In short, pain is not an unmediated response to an injury. Rather, it is a multidimensional phenomenon (Hanser, 2010: 858, citing Melzack, 2001: 1379), which means that pain is a topic for cultural sociology. How, in other words, may the mechanisms by which ascending pain signals reach the brain and come to be processed mediate, modify and heighten, or diminish, experienced pain? In earlier work I have considered these issues, suggesting that:

> music can modify pain because of how it is coupled or linked to things outside of individuals and to things that individuals do in tandem with attending to/making music. These things include social connotations (forms of relationship and other people), physical movements or postures (I relax or roll my shoulders in time with the music and start to feel easier) and forms of activity (memory, eating, thinking, day dreaming). All of these things are part of the apparatus of how music works. I use the term apparatus here as I used it earlier in this chapter when speaking of other forms of sensory 'illusion'. The difference is that now the distinction between 'illusion' and 'reality', the 'illusory' and 'real' bodies is more blurred. (DeNora, 2013: 110)

These examples of perception, its musical mediation, and the connection between musicalised perception and the reality of pain highlight some of the ways in which it seems justified to say that realities are neither virtual nor real – rather, they are '*virtually real*', drawn out of the potentially multiple ways in which things, sensations, experiences and meanings could become manifest. We have seen how the perception of realities depends upon artful practices and specific forms of action and perception. It is this practice that mediates between the multifarious possible realities and the seemingly resolute realities of apprehension. This link is minute, contingent and it involves precise activity on the part of presenters, users and observers. It involves materials and arrangements. It is, because of being dependent upon actual practice, fragile. And yet, paradoxically, indeed miraculously, realities are for all practical purposes produced and reproduced, shared and stabilised in often unproblematic, seemingly united ways. How does this occur? It is now time to examine, again through case study examples, how realities come to be built and shared, how the transmission of stabilised realities occurs, and how that practice involves the alignment of people, actions, perceptions and things. Thus, in the next and final chapter I turn to examples that highlight the multimedia crafting of our senses of reality.

9

THE SENSE OF REALITY: HERE, NOW, ARTFULLY, PRAGMATICALLY AND WITH CONSEQUENCES

To sum up the key points so far: realities are often multiple, and they are realised through artful practices that weave together words, acts, objects, meanings, perceptions and people. These practices are conditioned by what materials can be found to afford, by previous practice and by happenstance. They are not achieved necessarily willingly but they may come to configure what it is that individuals will perceive, expect and feel. Realities, then, are virtually real; that is, they are renditions of what is 'out there' around us and what confronts our senses at any given time. At the same time, culture does not predetermine how we make reality (for how then could we explain changes in what we deem the real?). For culture is, itself, a matter to be realised through instantiation and within specific circumstances, *somewhere*. Thus culture – artefacts, tools, sensory objects, meanings, customs, scripts and codes – is the mediator through which realities come to make sense to us but only in part. These cultural materials cannot, on their own, govern sense-making or instruct us about what to do; rather they offer partial or incomplete instructions – they are open-ended, flexible and related to what we do, with varying degrees of tension. Sometimes that tension is weak, other times so strong that it may seem that our action or knowledge of the world is automatic, even 'natural', as if to use a musical metaphor, we are 'singing from the same hymnbook'. As we now turn, in this chapter, to a consideration of how that mutual attunement is achieved, it makes sense, perhaps, to begin with an example of a highly tuned situation, namely, Alfred Schutz's treatment of 'making music together'.

CASE STUDY   Schutz on 'Making Music Together'

Alfred Schutz (1951) considered how music offers a form of (shared) 'meaningful context' of communication between composer and listener that transcends the need for concepts or words. He poses the performer as the intermediary for that process and considers the social relations of performing which he suggests are possessed of a 'highly complicated structure' (1951: 76); he describes how he is interested in exploring how we orient to others within a 'living present', how we manage to be synchronised in outer (e.g., clock) and inner (e.g., experiential) time, and how through a mutual tuning-in we experience a shared world.

It is important to realise that Schutz was not, primarily, concerned with founding a sociology of music through this study but rather, as he put it:

> it can be hoped that a study of the social relationships connected with the musical process may lead to some insights valid for many other forms of social intercourse. (1951: 76)

This point needs to be developed. Schutz himself clarifies things later on in his essay, suggesting that, 'the analysis of the social relationship involved in making music together might contribute to a clarification of the tuning-in relationship and the process of communication as such' (p. 96). In other words, Schutz's ambition is to learn about how it is that human beings can come to share a finely honed communicative world which is the world in which sense is made. Schutz's essay is useful because he describes some of the ways that human interaction is not simply rule-following (like playing chess) but rather he suggests that we cannot presuppose the 'rules of the game' as 'given from the outset' (1951: 77). His interest is in what he describes as the 'precommunicative social relationship' which he suggests comes to the foreground in various non-linguistic forms of human activity where, as he puts it, we can have 'the common experience of living simultaneously in several dimensions of time' (p. 94), such as:

> marching together, dancing together, making love together, or making music together and this last-named activity will serve as an example for analysis in the following pages. It is hoped that this analysis will in some measure contribute to clarification of the structure of the mutual tuning-in relationship, which originates in the possibility of living together simultaneously in specific dimensions of time. It is also hoped that the study of the particular communicative situation within the musical process will shed some light on the nonconceptual aspect involved in any kind of communication. (1951: 79)

Beginning with the notion that the musical score does not convey everything necessary for its performance ('all musical notation remains of necessity vague and open to manifold interpretations and it is up to the reader or performer to decipher the hints in the score and to define the approximation' [p. 84]), Schutz goes on to explore how, despite the potentially polysemic score and its capacity for multiple meanings, a coherent interpretation is performed. Interpretation, as Schutz puts it (p. 87) is 're-creation'. That re-creation is in turn the means by which mutually oriented, inner or experiential time (*durée*) is produced (the 'vivid present' [p. 93]) and thus the means for achieving a pre-communicative being-together in time.

From here, Schutz describes that the means for achieving coherence, for working as one in other words on 'a' version of the piece, is detailed, highly attuned performative practice, close listening and intimate awareness of the other. As Schutz puts it:

> each coperformer's action is oriented not only by the composer's thought and his relationship to the audience but also reciprocally by the experiences in inner and outer time of his fellow performer. Technically, each of them finds in the music sheet before him only that portion of the musical content which the composer has assigned to his instrument for translation into sound. Each of them has, therefore, to take into account what the other has to execute in simultaneity. He has not only to interpret his own part, which as such remains necessarily fragmentary, but he has also to anticipate the other player's interpretation of his – the other's – part and, even more, the other's anticipations of his own execution … Both share not only the inner *durée* in which the content of the music played actualizes itself; each, simultaneously, shares in vivid present the other's stream of consciousness in immediacy. This is possible because making music together occurs in a true face-to-face relationship – inasmuch as the participants are sharing not only a section of time but also a sector of space. The other's facial expressions, his gestures in handling his instrument, in short all the activities of performing, gear into the outer world and can be grasped by the partner in immediacy. (1951: 94–5)

Schutz concludes by describing how, as he sees it, only a small number of performers can manage to coordinate in this highly attuned, intimate manner. When the numbers increase, a 'leader' – a conductor, for example – is required (p. 95). The tuning-in relationship that Schutz explores in this essay, he suggests, is presupposed by all communication (p. 96).

ORIENTATION: MUTUAL OR MULTIPLE?

We have explored earlier the importance of being together in time and I will return to it below (see the discussion of Trevarthen's 2010 work, 'What is it Like to Be a Person Who Knows Nothing?'). Schutz poses the performer as the intermediary for composer-listener communication and considers the social relations of performing which he suggests are possessed of a 'highly complicated structure' (1951: 76). He then describes how he is interested in exploring how we orient to others within a 'living present', how we manage to be synchronised in outer (e.g., clock) and inner (e.g., experiential) time, and how through a mutual tuning in we experience a shared world. His focus on being together in time highlights a key feature of how it is that we make and consolidate sensible realities together, that is, realities that involve shared or mutually oriented perceptual habits and shared inner time or *durée*. But most of the time in the course of a day, week or lifetime, we do not 'make music' together in this highly prescribed way. By contrast, our interactions and reality projects involve a looser weave. That is to say that most action is not very similar to the performance of musical scores where so much of our every sound, and by implication, bodily movement, is preordained (pitch, rhythm, volume, pace, texture, sometimes even timbre). The example of performing a classical piece is one in which performers have not only a pre-scripted text (albeit only partially instructive, only partially spelled out) but also, often, hundreds of hours of rehearsal time devoted to a specific score, devising plans and strategies for that score's handling.

Thus the example of fine-grained attunement that Schutz presents with the case of music performance lies at one end of a continuum: at the other end are situations where there is an absence of mutual orientation, no sense of shared situation in time, and where there is confusion and cross-cutting forms of communicative activity. Somewhere in the middle, perhaps, is what happens on most occasions of daily life, and this middle ground involves forms of action that are more improvisatory, messier and more contingent; they are forms where there is no guiding text or script but where that script itself has to be produced, as it were, on the hoof.

So, for example, you and I may believe we are oriented to the 'same' situation and set of meanings; we may go away from an activity believing that the occasion was shared, and yet we may have quite divergent understandings – at least or until we begin to 'hash out the details'. Then, as we begin to delve more deeply things may go awry because of the inevitably indexical character of all meaning (e.g., 'but I thought we were talking about …'). On the other hand, we may develop certain practices for containing potential troubles in mutual understanding. We may, as Saferstein puts it (2007: 443), resort to a kind of 'grey boxing' of certain matters, so that the semblance of mutual orientation can continue unimpeded – albeit with varying consequences (see also Acord, 2014).

Even in bureaucratic organisations where texts and procedures are made explicit (think of those interminable 'rule books' that many of us, students, teachers, administrators and researchers in academic sectors encounter on a daily basis), there is often a far greater degree of mess, ambiguity and confusion than is officially acknowledged. To pursue the musical metaphor, knowing the score involves actual work of composition, not just co-performance. Mark Jacobs' study of legal procedure and its ambiguities, *Screwing the System and Making it Work* (the title was taken from an informant who described the work in these terms), helps to illustrate the everyday mess that is the setting of reality's creation.

CASE STUDY   Jacobs on *Screwing the System and Making it Work*

In a closely observed study of probation officers and juvenile offenders, Jacobs describes how dedicated court workers sought to do 'their best' for the young people in their charge and in the face of considerable 'mess'. Jacobs paints a picture of chronic disappointment and a systemically disorganised system of juvenile justice. He observes how:

> Despite the varied and diffuse nature of children's problems, related public agencies invoke the vague and contradictory mandates of federal law in defining their cognate competencies and responsibilities in narrowly specialized ways. (1990: 4)

Here Jacobs shows us law-in-action: the maze of contradictory mandates is negotiated and, in that negotiation, competencies and responsibilities come to be defined in the here and now of specific cases. Thus, we can see a specific place (somewhere), characterised not only by too much reality (the red tape) but also too many realities ('contradictory mandates'), and Jacobs' close study of agency workers illuminates how duties come to be discharged *despite* endemic disorganisation. The study describes how court workers' jobs involve overcoming various matters that are meant to govern how they work but instead impede their work – contradictory mandates; conflicting overseers such as judges, parents and lawyers; limited time, energy and official evasion. This overcoming, Jacobs shows, involves the use of alternative, non-official, unconventional methods, such as tapping informal networks so as to make the 'system' work (or look as if it is working).

(Continued)

(Continued)

As such Jacobs' study explores the ways in which court decisions are produced through situated, artful and negotiated practices. Jacobs' work thus highlights how the official description of an organisation and its workings cannot be taken at face value. By contrast, Jacobs' work shows us the ways in which organisational actors make meaning within the confines of perceived, often-shifting and amorphous, contradictory organisational constraints. In particular, his study observes the ways in which court workers tap narrative genres to account for their casework and how this tapping, or drawing-in of cultural forms to the frame of court work, enhances motivation and bestows meaning on an otherwise potentially absurd situation. Jacobs' court workers thus effectively enact the reality of workplace organisation through the ways they circumvent it. Circumventing official descriptions and officially encoded procedures ('screwing the system') is, in other words, the way to make the system 'work'. But work how? As Jacobs sums it up, case workers artfully produce narratives about their charges and their work, and these narratives create:

> the possibility for purposeful action by indicating how a prescribed course of treatment can lead to redemptive rebirth ... the casework narrative is no mere 'account,' repairing a breach on the surface of social order. Rather its function is much more profound: to affirm meaning and motivation essential to social control on a number of different levels ... the casework narrative offers symbolic resolution to the structural contradiction of probation casework.

> Unfortunately however, the resolution is only symbolic, and dysfunctional in its practical consequences ... Probation officers tend to enforce their narratives rather than the law; they remove children from home not only for new offenses but also for deviations from their cast roles. (Jacobs, 1990: 262)

Jacobs' study highlights how social actors often *do their best* to make things accountable, meaningful and orderly under often inhospitable, muddled, or otherwise confusing circumstances, and when the task of producing order may seem nigh impossible. Through these everyday efforts, seemingly unsung and often mundane, the sense of reality is enacted and re-enacted as a rhetorical project (see also Gusfield, 2000) and the 'system' continues to inspire belief, indeed loyalty. As such, Jacobs reveals a different account of how 'reality', in this case organisational, is put together and how those diverse practices of assembly are usually invisible, veiled by the very general categories that they have scrambled to sustain.

Thus Jacobs' study reminds us that in many walks of life, and even in bureaucratic organisations in which there would appear to be a rule for everything, actors do not so much 'follow the score' or adhere to a picture (a map, a rule book or a treaty), as they *compose* that score, *draw* that picture, *write* those rules, all the while behaving as if (and perhaps sometimes even believing that) they were merely working 'according to spec'. We are back at the point developed in Chapter 6: namely, it is possible to see a reflexive, mutually constituted relationship between general categories (the organisation's ethos, rules and procedures) and individual instances (needing to deal with this task, here and now). But we have added something new and that new point needs to be clarified now. It is that if the general (the rules of the organisation, a category of being such as male or female) is not all that it is cracked up to be; if general forms take definition from those things that are meant to be their instances, then the reality of those general things itself becomes a matter that is achieved. It too must be made sensible in and through the 'artful practices' that draw together instances and categories, all the while acting as if that relationship were unproblematic, perhaps automatic and axiomatic.

It is here that we begin to appreciate the religious undertones in Durkheim's *Elementary Forms* – that is, we can begin to glimpse our ontological assumptions about what 'is' as part of a faith in reality. That faith is itself part of what sustains our sense of reality; it is part of the practice by which attention and doubt is deflected from the objects that are deemed to be reality. But it is also integral to what we might now call the transubstantiation of reality, the moment or zero-hour of action in which things become real. There is, in other words, a magic here, but that magic is entirely practical in terms of how it is effected. And transubstantiation is the process by which (as with the bread and the wine) the materials and the time of the here and now *become*, or are transformed into, the there and then; it is the moment in which they are indistinguishable, in which they seem as one. We experience, I submit, many of these minor miracles in the course of daily existence. They become evident once we are willing to slow down and take a look. Before the reader begins to suspect that I have ventured into a form of metaphysics, it is worth noting that others, most notably those who are concerned with what is sometimes called 'sensuous scholarship' and with a focus on actor networks and arrangement, have also noted that making sense of reality involves something akin to religious communion, as something that people make (craft) together. As Vannini et al. observe (also citing Hennion [2004, 2007], Fine [1995] and Ingold [2000]):

aesthetic transaction is a creative 'joint act' (see Blumer, 1969): an emergent, joint somatic act that bespeaks of the creative sensuous sociality of self and the transformative power of socio-somatic relationships. Thinking of sensing as a joint somatic act, rather than thinking about atomistic sensations and individualized perceptions that record external matter and translate them into mental schemata and the register of language, allows us to understand the senses as conscious, reflexive skills we use as part of our dwelling-in-the-world-with-others ... (2010: 388)

Thus, the 'everyday' is never 'ordinary'. It is the site where the extraordinary achievement of 'dwelling-in-the-world-with-others' is achieved. Making sense of reality is the means for that end and it can thus be seen as a form of devotion. From this conclusion, it is possible to develop a form of enquiry focused in on actors who are 'doing their best', tapping whatever resources are at hand in the real-time endeavour of everyday action to create realities, which in turn offer different bases for continuation, shared action and contact, in the world. This action involves fending off confusion, sorting out muddle, and managing to do and be in common and in real-time situations that, even when contended, involve mutual reality-commitments (e.g., we are here together now and disputing). It is worth considering another, perhaps yet more extreme example of how actors do their best to achieve this type of ordered contact, sometimes when in fact they may know nothing about culture and have no command of language. If Schutz's model of musical action stands at one end of a continuum (very tightly knit, ritually prescribed forms of reality production), psychologist Colwyn Trevarthen's (1977) description of mother–infant vocalisation might reasonably be positioned at the other end. The kind of music-making studied by Trevarthen goes beyond situations where musical scores are co-performed. It describes by contrast situations where mutual orientation and situation are collaboratively and locally produced, emergent from the ongoing moment-by-moment production of shared sound. It shows just how much of a sense of reality can be made, and just how little pre-existing culture is required since culture can be both made and acquired from what, for at least one or more participants, is initially an almost blank slate.

CASE STUDY   Trevarthen on 'What is it Like to Be a Person Who Knows Nothing?'

As Trevarthen, who has been examining mother-infant interaction for nearly four decades, observes (2010: 129), 'even newborns exhibit the exuberance and extravagance of proprioceptively regulated agency, or

> poly-rhythmic subjectivity, that is uniquely characteristic of all humans, and that animates the gesture narratives of musical sound'. Trevarthen documents how 'examples of extremely close coordinations of the infant's rudimentary vocalizations of pleasure or excitement with the baby talk of the mother are everywhere to be seen. Apparently, both partners are participating in a single rhythmic beat, as in music' (Trevarthen, 1977: 102).
>
> Trevarthen describes how the infant and mother/carer are not drawn into some external image or set of parameters of synchronic conduct but produce it locally in relation to each other. Basic vocalisations come to be entrained and offered as a basis for relationship, the proto-methods for language development and adult forms of communication. He concludes that:
>
>> the proto-cultural intelligence that can be attributed to a one-year-old infant, which comes to a rich imaginative ripeness in the next two years, with the intersubjective intentions and perceptions that it depends on, can be already found in the active agency and sociable awareness of an alert and contented newborn. (2010: 130)

Trevarthen's observations highlight how the question of what keeps us orderly needs to be extended to the human ability to look for and produce order even with the scarcest of resources (no verbal capacity, no knowledge of rules or scripts, but working with what is available and building on those resources over time). Here, in other words, there is mutual attunement, of the kind that Schutz described. There is also the creation of mutual orientation (interest in the ongoing production and exchange of gesture over time). There is not, however, the performance of a pre-scripted work. A good deal of our reality creation is improvised. Moreover, it is possible to create a sense of shared reality without language, without, that is, actually defining anything, and without naming the meanings of what is being done. Too much, perhaps, is made of meaning in social life, too little, perhaps, of coordinated, physical and material forms of action and their connection to preverbal, aesthetic orientation in real time. Somewhere in the middle of these extremes is the kind of expressive, mutually oriented action that takes place in relation to what perhaps might best be understood as quasi-culture: our half-understandings of how culture works, our half-formulated impulses and orientations in relation to images, gestures, habits and other 'systems' of meaning. We act, not within culture, but in relation to a sense of culture, a sometimes fragmented or faint or imagined 'memory' of how things 'ought' to be or how things most feel right. In so doing we are not enacting pre-given codes but enacting those codes through forms of action that would seem but to deploy them (see the point above about transubstantiation).

It is in this complicated sense, then, that we can situate the 'social performance' perspectives within cultural sociology. People do indeed, 'individually or in concert, display for others the meaning of their social situation' (Alexander et al., 2006: 32) but, as McCormick describes it, the concern with enactment is a concern with 'how collective representations are *conjured to construct the context of performance* and how these, in turn, guide the interpretation of performances enacted' (McCormick, 2009: 7, emphasis mine). Key here in the argument I have been developing is that performances involve the two-way enactment of individual performance (the here and now of what we do) and the background, collective representations or codes of what this doing means, its significance and sense of participation in some more general sense of reality. The 'conjuring' that McCormick mentions, in other words, is enactment, the act of creating seemingly firm connections between the this, here and now and the that, there and then. As Hennion describes it, this enactment is what 'holds us together'; it provides opportunities for connection and contact with others, including our most intimate forms of contact. Perhaps nowhere is this point better underlined than in the recent reappraisals of music therapy (Aigen, 2005; Ansdell and Pavlicevic, 2010; Procter, 2011; Stige et al., 2010): the recognition that the mutual creation of sound environments that constitute a session is, simultaneously, the making of relation and thus the remaking of identity as you make sounds in response to mine and I to yours, and as our mutual sound production constitutes an aesthetic environment within which we are being, here, now and which we can reflect upon later, there, then. In everyday-life encounters, recent work on the materiality of intimate relations serves to underline this point.

CASE STUDY   Wilson-Kovacs on intimacy and materiality

In a study that drew upon in-depth interviews with 34 women living in large and small cities in the UK, Dana Wilson-Kovacs (2007, 2009, 2010) explored how, as she puts it, 'at a mundane level, erotic affinities are created and sustained via cultural repertoires, and especially those drawing upon the use of material culture' (2007: 181). Intimate situations, relationships and forms of erotic agency, in other words, were crafted through the artful mobilisation of varied materials in ways that drew 'props' and users together into the 'rendering of sexual personas' (Wilson-Kovacs, 2007: 181). These materials helped to create, as respondents described it, a sense of occasion and scenic specificity. They helped, in other words, to enact intimacy and types of intimacy (within folksonomies as offered by respondents, say, 'the quickie', 'something special', etc.).

Wilson-Kovacs explored how the materials used to set the scene for intimate conduct were arranged such that they offered cues to the type of sexual encounter ('raunchy', 'romantic') and that facilitated respondents' own emotional work as they geared themselves up for forms of sexual encounter. As she puts it:

> the largely unacknowledged expressive work accompanying the ritual organization of sexual closeness (Wilson-Kovacs 2007), is seen as an indication of one's commitment to a relationship and a partner, as well as a mirror to one's identity. It is symptomatic of a gendered, emotional and verbal middle class habitus through which women sustain and reproduce dominant configu-rations of intimacy (Ilouz 1997, Reay 2005). Alongside such affec-tive elements, all intimate histories share a procedural order that involves the mobilisation of various resources ... (2010: 223)

Wilson-Kovacs' respondents described how they engaged in the craft of configuring intimacy and the role of objects in constituting different intimate realities:

> Not only are some items recognized as more effective than others in fuelling erotic fantasies, but taste is identified as the skill with which various props are combined for the appropriateness of each occasion. Aesthetic deliberations are at work not only in choosing appropriate articles of lingerie but also in integrating them in inti-mate scenarios. Keeping unwritten logs of occasions and items is typical for the ways that respondents use lingerie and distinguish between 'routine' undertakings and 'special' episodes. (2010: 223-4)

As with lingerie, so too the bedroom and the body, itself, is a rendition:

> Making the body sexually attractive depends on a combination of successful time allocation, readiness to embark on this transformation, and available resources. Most importantly, it is circumscribed by aesthetic judgement, as Gabrielle, a thirty-six-year-old podiatrist notes:

> I get an idea of what I like and what I look like when I try things on. I suppose to a certain extent I have preconceived ideas of what I should wear. I mean cheap lacy bras, forget it, but having said this I do have a range of things I wear ... I can do slut one night and virginal the next ... (Wilson-Kovacs, 2007: 188)

Wilson-Kovacs' research thus highlights how material objects, such as lingerie, home décor, candles, lighting, flowers, literature, art, music (see also DeNora, 2011 [1997], 2000), film and visual media, pornography, sex toys, food and drink, are drawn into the vortex of a potentially erotic or intimate occasion so as to make that occasion an *intimate* one. She also describes how this arrangement practice does not merely seek to invoke pre-existing codes that offer, as it were, a menu of potential intimate forms or scenarios. Rather, Wilson-Kovacs shows us how acts that mobilise materials do so in ways that structure forms of interaction and subjectivity. And materials themselves are mercurial symbolic things – their affordances, their meanings and significance may shift from moment to moment as they, themselves, are recontextualised. Material objects do not, in other words, contribute to situation definition in any mechanical sense because their own realities are themselves subject to instantiation in the here and now. A chair, for example, can become a table but it is also an aesthetic object and its aesthetic properties are or can be highly plastic, for example exquisitely beautiful one moment, ugly the next, depending upon many other emergent contextualising factors.

Wilson-Kovacs' research also chimes with more recent discussions of how objects work to promote wellbeing, and how the process by which objects are found and introduced to settings can be characterised. For example, using a qualitative-survey interview method with 65 respondents from eight countries, Paul Camic (2010) suggests that we can think about similar issues in relation to the discovery of 'found objects' (i.e., other people's trash). The process of this finding, as he puts it, 'involves the interaction of aesthetic, cognitive, emotive, mnemonic, ecological, and creative factors in the seeking, discovery, and utilization of found objects' (Camic, 2010: 81). Finding and placing objects, then, is part, Camic suggests (following Dissanayake, 1988), of making things 'special' (including making the found object special – its status reassignment from junk to art). The act of making special is in turn empowering because it:

> requires the finder to develop a symbolic meaning, and sometimes a functional use, for the object that goes beyond its present situation as culturally labeled detritus while simultaneously responding to its current physical and aesthetic elements. When the found object is seen by the finder as a symbol representing another entity (e.g., when an old blue bottle with foreign lettering comes to symbolize far away intrigue, mystery, and sophistication), support is given to what Dittmar (1992) described as socially constructing a material identity for the object. Expanding on Dittmar's use of a social interactionist perspective, the results of the present study support the possibility that the entire found object process – finding, reclassifying, and reusing objects – becomes a symbol of identity for the finder.

This supports Digby's (2006) argument that individuals make use of salvaged objects as souvenirs, which are no longer part of the commodity cycle, to rework and construct individual and social identities. (Camic, 2010: 90)

Wilson-Kovacs' and Camic's work shed light on how the discovery and arrangement of sensory and aesthetic objects in domestic settings in turn create ecologies that afford action and experience. Similarly, Pink has described how 'a domestic aesthetic can be conceptualised as part of a constantly shifting place-event constituted through constellations of these everyday things and mundane practices' (2012: 67). These understandings of home-atmospherics do not judge what people do when they create these constellations and they do not seek to impose the researcher's own responses to these constellations. So, for example, one would not as a researcher insert one's own feelings or interpretations of material constellations – as can happen when interview data is elevated into narratives about an individual's way of living, the '*What* does this home décor tell us about this person' question, though they might be concerned with the sustainability of a particular arrangement – e.g., in terms of the social, natural or economic resources that it takes to keep it in place, as Pink (2004) describes. By contrast, Wilson-Kovacs, Camic and Pink are concerned with processes, that is, with investigating the often non-verbal, pre-cognitive or tacit acts of furnishing, understood as the question of *how* objects are drawn into and maintained within scenarios of action. That project, with its focus on how, is concerned with what actors do in real time, what they introduce or remove, how they position and combine objects, when they gather many objects, and when they clear objects away or decline to collect them. In short, it is concerned with how we *curate* the situations of everyday life. These are key themes too in the so-called 'new sociology of art' (Witkin, 1994; Witkin and DeNora, 1997; de la Fuente, 2007; Acord and DeNora, 2008; Sutherland and Acord, 2007; Acord, 2010); that they apply equally to the enactment of experience in everyday life merely highlights the artfulness of that experience. It is in that artfulness, the crafting of ways of being together, making contact, proceeding through time in relation to others, things, ourselves, that we make sense of what could otherwise be a confusing and swirling mess of possible worlds and ways of being. At times the worlds that we make sense of draw us together tightly (for example, Schutz's example of re-creating the musical score). At other times those worlds are loosely woven. What matters is the attempt to do the weaving, how and with what, and how this weaving allows for certain consequences (opportunities for action and experience, for ways of being and doing together) to emerge.

It will be obvious to some readers that in describing how the sense of reality is enacted and realised through the pulling of things together

I am outlining a perspective closely associated to those discussed by many others in relation to actor network theory, and to its more recent configuration in theories of enactment and assembly. It is important again to underline how this theory does not necessitate an understanding of the assembly process as a mechanical one since all aspects of the things that are drawn together mutually constitute each other in relation to each other in the here and now of their mobilisation, in much the same way that I 'perform' meaning about the world when I speak, seemingly, about its pre-existing status (for example, if I say, 'I now pronounce you husband and wife' or 'I believe it is warm in this room'). In other words, objects, words, tools, actions or aesthetic media, in themselves, can create neither experience nor capacity. But pulled together and in real time they can make sense or structure experience and capacity, allowing it to take shape *this* way, not that way. Thinking about human capacity as the outcome of our social-material-aesthetic and practical arrangements draws the study of reality and how it is produced into one of the most ethically, and scientifically, important areas of study for the human sciences, namely the study of distributed ability/disability understood as distributed opportunities for being well.

CASE STUDY Langer on ageing as a culturally produced condition

In 1979, Ellen Langer and her research associates set out to test the impact of environmental arrangements on wellbeing in later life. As Langer put it, the work sought to develop a 'psychology of possibility' (2009: 15). They designed a study where two groups of elderly men participated in two separate week-long retreats. Both groups of men spent a week living under conditions that sought, as closely as possible, to replicate conditions of life circa 1959, that is when these men were 20 years younger. This replication was achieved by furnishing the retreat environment with physical objects, technologies, furniture, reading matter, television programmes and photos of self and family all of no later than 1959. The group met to discuss events that took place in the 1950s, including sports events, political issues and the launch of the first US satellite; they listened to the music of Jack Benny and Nat 'King' Cole and read Leon Uris' *Exodus* and Philip Roth's *Goodbye, Columbus*. The only difference between the groups was that the first group were asked to function *as if they were living in the present*, namely 20 years younger and actually still living in the year 1959. They were asked to speak about the events discussed as if they were happening now, not to 'reminisce' about events but to try to 'let yourself be just who you were in 1959'. The second group, by contrast, were asked to use the past tense when discussing issues and self, to remember back, as it were, from the current standpoint of being old(er).

Participants were assessed before and after the study according to the following indicators of wellbeing: weight, dexterity, flexibility and vision (with and without eye glasses), sensitivity to taste, intelligence tests, visual memory tests, evaluation of appearance and self-evaluation. The study found a broad improvement in test scores in the first group – those participants who were living in the present of 1959 (talking in the present tense about the satellite launch, etc.). Langer and her associates concluded that the improvements in wellbeing commensurate with anti-ageing were linked to a kind of placebo effect, whereby the mind, triggered by the surroundings of 20 years earlier, led participants to believe they actually were 20 years younger. Mindfulness, Langer concluded, can affect how our bodies behave, how 'old' we are according to seemingly objective criteria.

While the implications of mindfulness, and the role of, as it were, mind over matter are important and intriguing – think back to the discussion of music and pain management in Chapter 8 – there are other issues that are also relevant here that underline the ways that individual matters (so-called 'internal' experience, wellbeing and orientation) take shape in relation to things that lie outside them. For example, Langer's study also highlights how culture and the built environment can diminish the ways in which people are, and behave in ways that are, deemed 'different', 'failing' or, in this case, 'old'. Langer's study shows how social environments can offer differential access to pleasure, joy and forms of ability, according to how they are furnished.

The question of how furnishing environments takes shape and how it can capacitate is also a question about for whom environments are designed, and this question, perhaps especially in relation to health, illness and disability, is an urgent one for cultural sociology. Mariko Hara's (2011) ethnographic research in and around a singing group for people living with dementia, their loved ones, carers and volunteers, highlights this point. Her work illustrates how culture not only triggers people's self-conceptions, but how a situation can be artfully, in this case musically, put together in ways that enhance togetherness and diminish the significant differences that might otherwise be magnified for those with/out dementia.

CASE STUDY   Hara on 'Singing for the Brain'

Taking a person-centred approach, Hara describes how participants (Laura and later Arnold) can be seen to undergo a kind of metamorphosis in real time:

> the SFTB sessions enable Laura to be a very different person from the Laura I met outside the sessions. In the sessions she is always very confident and cheerful when interacting with others, she is alert and accurate about the words she sings and easily follows the facilitator's instructions when it comes to challenging activities such as singing in parts. It seems that SFTB sessions allow her to reconnect to the enjoyment of being with others and the joy of taking the initiative. Out of this context, she is not as cheerful or confident as in the sessions. (Hara, 2011: n.p.)

Laura 'becomes' a more extrovert, joyful person within the temporal and spatial, highly crafted context of a 'Singing for the Brain' session. Within that context she finds sources of enjoyment, confidence and skill that, in other environments, elude her. It is worth noting that this point is by no means germane only to personal and cultural management of dementia. To the contrary, crafting musical environments has been shown by a growing body of researchers to be part of the care of self (DeNora, 2000) and an important part of salutogenics (Ruud, 2005 ; Batt-Rawden, 2006). In Laura's case, this sense of what kind of person she is or can be is emergent and takes shape *in situ*; it is achieved in relation to the social, cultural and material environment. Laura's 'disability' then is also more plastic than might otherwise seem: it takes shape in relation to cues, materials and the 'somewhere' of interactive occasions where capacities are fostered or suppressed.

These occasions are not governed cultural codes, categories, rules or images. Rather they are achieved through situated, artful practices. So, for example, Laura does not emerge as her former and more active, coherent self simply because she is sitting in a circle at a 'Singing for the Brain' session, or even because she is taking part in the singing of a particular song. Rather, her renewal is achieved through something much more complicated, more 'hand-crafted' by Laura and her peers:

> The way that a music therapeutic environment can affect one to become 'someone else' has also been discussed in community music therapy (Ansdell, 2002). Aasgaard (2000) has talked about how song creation in a paediatric oncology ward shifted one client's role from 'patient' to 'song maker' or 'creative person.' He defines this process as an 'ecological music therapy practice'. This

practice, in Bruscia's words, equates healthcare with the health of the social environment, 'helping an individual to become healthier is not viewed as a separate enterprise from improving the health of the ecological context within which the individual lives' (Bruscia, 1998, p. 229). The SFTB sessions are planned and carried out taking the limitations and the capacities of the members with dementia into consideration; however, the sessions do not target individual behavioural or emotional problems. Rather, Jessica and around 10 volunteers attempt to craft an inclusive structure, enlivened by group singing and the various relationships between all the participants, the so-called 'ecological context', which allowed Laura and Arnold to be 'uninhibited' and feel confident about themselves. In other words, this carefully crafted 'ecological context' offers them an opportunity to shift roles from 'people with dementia' to 'cheerful singers and dancers'. (Hara, 2011: n.p.)

Carefully crafting social situations of musical action can, in other words, offer new grounds for relating and action, new ways of perceiving people. Like the magic trick, attention is diverted from what (some) people cannot do (remember the date, the name of the Prime Minister) to, through participatory activity, what they can do and are doing which in turn is constructed in ways that give pleasure, and are enabling, to all. While not just any music would work for this purpose (there is no point in attempting, for example, to learn the Mozart *Requiem*, a previous favourite of one group member who used to sing in a high-level amateur choir), and while some aesthetic negotiation is undergone to find what will suit the purpose, it is important to note that it is not the presence of music *per se* but what is done with it *in situ*, emergently in time and in relation to other developments as they happen. This crafting, the joining together of repertoire, situated practices of introducing music, the order of play, style and associated physical positioning/movement activities together achieve something akin to magic, a set of circumstances which – for a time – transfigure participants (all of them, not just the ones who are 'living with dementia'), and in so doing enable relationships to be rekindled and enjoyed. As one participant put it, 'This is when I meet "old mum" ... Those moments are very important for me' (Hara, 2011: n.p.).

Hara's and Langer's work serve to highlight the area of (dis)ability studies as one of the best natural laboratories for examining how the (potentially always multiple) senses(s) of reality are achieved and how the production of virtually real realities are, simultaneously, the production of socially distributed forms of capacity. This area has been the subject of recent interest in social theory and in a form of theory that has been highly attentive to practice and to the material worlds. It reveals the actual 'realities' of dis/ability as rendered through specific arrangements of people, practices, meanings and things in space and time.

This project begins by thinking about the ways in which practices of knowing and sensory engagement are often embedded into objects and the situations in which objects are engaged. In his work on museum access, Kevin Hetherington (2002, 2003) has described how, when we are in the British Museum, we are meant to, as it were, look not touch the Parthenon Frieze, to experience it as a 'sight' using a visual mode of knowing that is distal, as opposed to the more proximal or close-up modes of touch or smell. These modes of knowing differentially configure the Museum's accessibility. They also stabilise the sense of sight as we assume it 'must' function and deflect alternative versions of what it might be to 'see' these sculptures.

CASE STUDY   Hetherington on touching at the museum

For example, Hetherington describes the experience of accompanying (visually impaired) Sarah on a visit to the British Museum where she touch-toured designated sculptures in the Graeco-Roman Gallery, all the while describing the experience to Hetherington:

> Sarah went around the gallery touching the sculptures and describing her experiences to me. In part, she was engaged in an act of identification, establishing for herself what each of the sculptures represented. But she was also fascinated by what she called 'the feel' and how it connected with her. The textures of the different kinds of stone that had been used and the variations in temperature were all equally important. As someone skilled in touch and reflexively knowledgeable about it, both as an everyday practice and as a practice associated with museum objects, she told me that she was sensitive to the texture of materials in varying ways depending on how she touched them, which hand she used, whether she made broad sweeping movements with her hands, or more local, detailed investigations with her fingertips. What she found she then also related to experience, mood, feelings and so on. (Hetherington, 2003: 105)

Hetherington goes on to describe how alternative means of experiencing the sculptures are provided for people who are 'visually impaired', capturing what he sees as the more tentative, more emergent and perhaps more intimate way of knowing the sculptures that the mode of touch affords, which he contrasts with the Museum's own Guidebook for the Blind:

To provide a book like the Second Sight of the Parthenon Frieze for the visually impaired is to acknowledge, in part, the importance that touch has for the visually impaired but it is to do so from the standpoint of an optical perspective and a politics of difference that treats all forms of recognition as an issue of access through sight as the basis for representation. (2002: 202)

If, then, within a moment of interaction or within a social world, we employ or are expected to employ one mode or practice rather than another, the very practice of 'how' to know, how to experience, will enact the virtually real reality of dis/ability. (Think of how the fox, in Aesop's tale, avenges the stork, who had invited the fox to dinner but then served the soup in a beaker so tall and narrow that the fox could not sup. The fox issues a return invitation but this time serves the soup in shallow saucers, and this time the stork, with his long and narrow beak, is incapacitated. In each case, the condition of ability was enabled or disabled in relation to material artefacts, the dishes used to contain the soup [see DeNora, 2006].)

But Hetherington's point is yet more subtle and more critical. He is concerned with how the sense of vision is interpellated (brought into being, identified) through technologies that reconstitute touch as if it were a prosthetic form of sight, a 'supplement' to 'an impaired and unfinished body'. Touch is used, in other words, as a proxy for what cannot be seen with the eyes rather than 'more positively through an understanding of skilled, sensitive touch' (2003: 113). As such, Hetherington shows us just how deeply into the body our virtually real realities can be seen to penetrate, and just how deeply from that body they are drawn while drawing the body from which they seem to emanate.

In *Rethinking Dis/ability* (2010) Schillmeier suggests that we need 'to make the social of disability traceable' (2010: 5). He proposes a 'new empiricism' of 'the very specificities of everyday practices of dis/ablement', a focus that is attentive to what he calls the 'complex and contingent scenarios of dis/abilities that create enabling and disabling (or, as he puts it, 'dis/abling') practices. Put in different words, Schillmeier seems to be suggesting that dis/abilities arise from combinations of material objects, technologies and practices which distribute ease and/or troubles in daily life within social spaces. From this position, then, it is possible to consider the everyday acts that, 'wittingly or unwittingly, fabricate people as disabled or enabled' (2010: 6).

Thus, Schillmeier's study highlights a direction within (dis)ability studies that is concerned with how disabilities and abilities emerge in relation to figured grounds, in relation to arrangements of objects, ways of seeing, technologies, meanings and practices such that any so-called disability, from visual impairment to dementia to immobility, can be understood to exist only if it is set in context of these arrangements. Culture, in other words, renders (dis)ability as a 'now you see it, now you don't' phenomenon. It is about what elsewhere Schillmeier (2008) describes as the time–spaces of independence and dis/ability. By this term, Schillmeier means a focus on how the reality of socio-physical condition, such as that of being 'blind', is produced temporally and spatially, moment to moment through the ways that time and space are mediated through material/social/cultural acts. These acts produce, in other words (and note the connection to Mol and her 'body multiple'), multiple 'blind' times and spaces. The reality of 'blindness', in other words, emerges in relation to where we are, what we do, how we do, or may be expected to 'do'; and the modalities associated with that doing and the technical and cultural modalities that afford this doing produce what we take to be independence or impairment.

As an example, consider the health-status of being physically mobile. Mobility is a relational state and a meaningful state; it is not 'merely' a property of individuals but rather emerges from a series of practices and interactions with the built environment. This interaction – between humans and objects and between humans and categories of meanings – will augment or diminish ability/disability according to how the built environment is organised (Freund, 2001). If curbs are converted into sloping surfaces, if traffic lights allow for longer crossing times at the 'walk' or 'green man' [*sic*] signs (or the aural signal that tells visually impaired people that it is safe to cross a road), if we do away with stairs, then the difference between wheelchair users and walkers is of less consequence. If, by contrast we raise curb height to three feet, we have not only created a barrier between those who are able to walk and those who aren't; we may also create a barrier between those who are able to climb and those who cannot. As with mobility, so too with hearing impairment, as the next case study illustrates.

Making Sense of Reality

CASE STUDY   Groce on *Everyone Here Spoke Sign Language*

Nora Groce's (2006 [1988]) study highlights how hearing impairment was, for all practical purposes, inconsequential in 19th-century Martha's Vineyard, an island off the east coast of the US. Because the material practices of work did not require spoken interaction and because, in her titular phrase, 'everyone here spoke sign language' the social impact of physical conditions, such as not being able to hear, was greatly diminished. It was further diminished through the practices by which work was organised (spoken talk was not necessary) and through social practices that minimised the need for an audible world. Groce's study does not seek to deny the reality of hearing impairment. But she shows how that reality can take different forms according to how it is drawn into proximity with social and technical arrangements, forms of action and communicative conventions, and it can be seen to grow or diminish in significance in relation to these things. The meaning of the general category, 'hearing impaired', and more broadly, 'disability', in other words, is variable; it is dependent upon, or rather emerges from, its relation to cultural and crafted arrangements, and on this small island in the 19th century, with this group of people, the reality of being hearing impaired was that it did not deny a person access to widely shared practices – of work, talk, leisure and connection. It is this realm where the symptoms associated with health/illness and ability/disability come to be manifest and matter, where they are lived as day-to-day 'realities'. Thus, instances and categories of disability become 'real' (i.e., socially significant as types of health and illness) through the ways that they take shape in relation to situations of practice.

The work I have been considering, in the final section of this chapter, examines how institutional, material set-ups can make a difference; can suppress a difference and draw individuals together in relation to what can be made to be in common; can actually fabricate (i.e., give substance to, substantiate) forms of ability/disability. They illuminate the reality-status of disability as emergent and they point, moreover, to how any identity status, including ones associated with physical characteristics, is nonetheless put together through artful practices of drawing together and tinkering with people and things, meanings and situations. We have seen, moreover, that physical symptoms themselves (or rather, the awareness of them, how they come to impinge on us) can also be transformed (e.g., the case of pain management and sensation discussed in Chapter 8). The reality of what is possible, and what is impossible, is now also opened up as a topic for sociology and as a challenge of daily life.

CASE STUDY   A sociology of the possible? Mukerji on the Canal du Midi

In her book *Impossible Engineering: Technology and Territoriality on the Canal du Midi* (2009), Chandra Mukerji considers matters not too

(Continued)

distant from Ellen Langer's concern with a 'psychology of possibility' that I discussed earlier. Building a long canal through the Languedoc region of France in the second half of the 17th century, so as to link the Mediterranean to the Atlantic (the largest engineering work and the biggest canal ever in the Western world), was a project that asserted 'territorial politics', the 'construction' of a 'new Rome' in the Ancient Regime of Louis XIV's France. In this sense, the creation of the canal provided an example of how technical and engineering achievements can be linked to and help to constitute political and economic power (see Mazzotti [2004] for a similar study of the mechanisation of olive oil in the 18th century). But what Mukerji describes is also about how this project was:

> not technically possible according to the formal engineering knowledge of the period. Some called it a work of the Devil; the entrepreneur who built it, Pierre-Paul Riquet, attributed its success to God; and propagandists touted it as a measure of the glory of Louis XIV. (Mukerji, 2009: xix)

And yet, the canal was made. That making involved artisans (including unsung women, later written out of the history, who knew about water management). It included those with a long-standing, abiding understanding (gentle empiricism) of local conditions. In company with engineers and planners these people worked together to combine otherwise fragmented, tacit and only half-remembered skills (dating back to Roman times) of knowing how to make water move. Their combined work and the collective effervescence of knowledge about hydraulics it created was what did the trick: together, cooperatively, improvisatorially, these participants tapped distributed knowledge, tinkered with materials and drew on (and drew out each other's) craft and skill. The result was more than the sum of its parts: the impossible became possible – the canal was built, it was a 'marvel', and Mukerji took a long boat down it in the 1990s as part of her research.

THINKING ABOUT (AN)AESTHETIC MATERIAL PRACTICES IN TIME

The study of how we make sense of reality is also the sociology of the possible. We have considered, in the last section of this chapter, a number of examples of how the 'impossible' can be converted into the possible, if not (following Aristotle) always the probable (given the nature of change, reorientation and resources involved). It is time, now, to conclude what I have to say, and I wish to do that through a last case study example.

I said at the outset to this book that music was 'good to think with' and I began this book with a case study from the musical work of Theodor Adorno. I will therefore end with a final example from research in socio-music studies, which also returns me, as the author, to my main research field. I think that music is good to think with because it is a non-verbal, often non-representative medium and one that does not much depend upon the sense of seeing, though of course that can be vital for some forms of music production, distribution and reception (watching for the downbeat of the conductor's baton; album covers and performer images; para-musical features of performance such as gesture). At the same time music is a highly material practice that involves instruments, notation devices, forms of embodied skill and situations of production and reception (from concert halls to kitchens to mobile music-listening while in transport). And music is a temporal medium, moreover one that depends upon, as we saw in the examples from Schutz and Trevarthen, doing things together in time.

CASE STUDY   Ansdell et al. on songs without words

Pam hits the xylophone hard with the beaters and throws them towards the piano, which they hit, causing the piano strings to vibrate. She shouts 'This fucking life!' and becomes very upset. (The therapist [Gary Ansdell] later finds out that the outburst was caused by her seeing the letter names on the xylophone spelling out abusive messages to her from an internal voice.) Immediately after the blow-up the therapist gently gets Pam to come to the piano, to sit beside him, and encourages her back into musical engagement again. She begins playing a few notes on the top of the piano, which leads into a short piano duet and then into shared singing with the therapist. Pam takes over the singing herself after a short time (accompanied by the therapist on the piano), becoming involved and expressive. The music seems to take her somewhere else. After the music cadences she sighs and says, 'That's better!' The entire episode has lasted just over four minutes. (Ansdell et al., 2010)

In this example of 'live' musical participation, music can be seen as a way of being - together. Here music is a great deal more than the producing and sharing of organised sound. It involves, as we saw in the

(Continued)

case study from Mukerji's work, a form of 'impossible engineering'; that is, the *collaborative, interactive, literally concerted drawing-together* of postures, mutual orientation and para-musical action (talk, movement, gesture and ancillary activities. It involves too materials and objects – pianos, xylophones, beaters – which may themselves be imbued with connotations, personal or historical and cultural (for example, the piano may be understood as 'the instrument my father played'; or as a 'posh' instrument, the xylophone is associated in popular and classical musical culture with skeletons and the musical macabre). It is artful practice and it remakes the sense of what transpires between these participants, Pam and Gary, and how each of them is involved in deploying and displaying a knack for this musical production which is the contact between them. (In this way we see how musical communicative action offers what Procter calls 'proto-social capital', or a means by which people can become connected, and a foundation upon which other forms of connection can accumulate [Procter, 2011].) It could have been otherwise and that otherwise could have led to very different outcomes, short and longer term.

Through this artful practice – in this case beyond words albeit culminating in words ('that's better') – relationships are established, quickly and for a time such that, in an almost mythic way, it can seem as if everything 'fits' (Rojek, 2011: 15); that all is 'well', in the sense that the different aspects of this scene (talk, movement, gesture, ancillary activities, objects and participants) are perceived as complementing, facilitating and therefore validating each other. The little 'cap' or 'coda' of narrative offered by Pam is both enabled and supported by this mutual complementarity *and* enhances that complementarity as it enacts a sense of 'better-ness'. In this sense, we can see how complex and how minute is the artfulness of making 'what happened' *in and as it is being made,* and also in this sense we can see how the sense of reality as it is made and remade is consequential. In this example, a lot happened in, seemingly, a very short time.

MAKING SENSE IN TIME, CHARITABLY?

The work we have considered in the final section of this book, by Langer, Hara, Hetherington, Schillmeier, Groce, Mukerji and Ansdell et al., shows how a great deal of virtually real reality can be built around a detail in ways that are transformative, that heighten or diminish its significance, its reality status. The literatures on disability and on wellbeing show us how it is virtually possible to eradicate (for a time, in a place) dis-eased aspects of reality such as hearing or visual impairment, dementia, age or mental distress. These literatures also show how it is possible to create ecologies in which is it difficult to sustain that dis-ease and thus they address the famous titular question of Langdon Winner's (1980) essay, 'Do Artifacts Have Politics?' And so, once we understand how they are made, their virtually real status, we can begin to have at least an inkling of insight into how to remake them differently. To say this by no means also implies that all people will then be 'able' to do precisely the same things as all others (be able to sing the soprano line in the Mozart *Requiem*, be able to see, walk, hear, or feel at ease, or have the skills needed to build a canal in which water flows uphill). But it *does* imply that these differences can become more or less real in their significance to us; that their locations 'in', and differences of degree between, individuals may vary spatially/temporally (some days I may be able to sing Mozart, other days not); and, most powerfully, that their very ontological status as objective 'things' in the world can be re-specified such that, for example, what it means to sing, see, have skill or hear can be reformulated (I 'hear' or 'see' through the sense of touch and my environment does not make that way of doing problematic). The ways that we make sense of reality are, in other words, variable, multiple, temporal, situated and connected to temporal and ecological situations of people, practices, situations, meanings and things. To examine that situation is to re-specify cultural sociology and Emile Durkheim's aphorism (to treat social facts as things): it is to examine the question of from where that 'thing-ness' comes. It is also to understand that in rearranging cultural forms we remainder – understood in Adorno's sense as noun *and* verb – different things.

In everyday life we make and remake ease and ability in every moment of every day, often and as a matter of routine. It is perhaps most clearly evident in relation to that which we love, when we tinker with an environment, a wording or a gesture, avoid certain situations, practices or things, and in so doing, manage to nurture that love – or its dignity, beauty, validity, comfort, pleasure, participation, peace, passion and sensed importance in our lives. The words I have just used are abstractions (or, Philip Larkin's word, blazons), but they are and can be made into realities through arrangement and rearrangement, through the artful practices that draw people, things and meanings together, the artful practices of *how* realities become real. From this perspective we can see how cultural worlds, and with them senses of reality, are ever in flux, subject to negotiation and renegotiation. At stake within this flux is nothing less than the 'real in its consequences' distribution of opportunities for action and experience. *Which* realities, then, deserve virtually to be real?

REFERENCES

Acord, Sophia (2010) Beyond the Head: The Practical Work of Curating Art. *Qualitative Sociology*, 33: 447–67.

Acord, Sophia (2014) Art Installation as Knowledge Assembly: Curating Contemporary Art. Tassos Zembylas (Ed), *Knowledge and Artistic Practices*. London: Routledge, 151–65.

Acord, Sophia and Tia DeNora (2008) Culture and the Arts: From Art Worlds to Arts-in-Action. *The Annals of the American Academy of Political and Social Science*, 619: 223–37.

Adorno, Theodor (1980) *The Philosophy of Modern Music*. New York: Seabury.

Adorno, Theodor (1997) *Aesthetic Theory*, G. Adorno and R. Tiedemann (Eds), R. Hullot-Kentor (Trans). Minneapolis: University of Minnesota Press.

Adorno, Theodor (2005) *Negative Dialectics*. New York: Continuum.

Aigen, Kenneth (2005) *Music-centered Music Therapy*. Gilsum, NJ: Barcelona Publishers.

Alexander, Jeffrey (2003) *The Meanings of Social Life: A Cultural Sociology*. Oxford: Oxford University Press.

Alexander, Jeffrey (2006) Cultural Pragmatics: Social Performance Between Ritual and Strategy. In Jeffrey Alexander, Bernhard Giesen and Jason Mast (Eds) *Social Performance: Symbolic Action, Cultural Pragmatics, and Ritual*. Cambridge: Cambridge University Press, pp. 1–91.

Alexander, Jeffrey and Jason L. Mast (2006) Introduction: Symbolic Action in Theory and Practice; The Cultural Pragmatics of Symbolic Action. In J. Alexander, B. Giesen and J. Mast (Eds), *Social Performance: Symbolic Action, Cultural Pragmatics, and Ritual*. Cambridge: Cambridge University Press, pp. 1–27.

Alexander, Jeffrey and Philip Smith (Eds) (1988) *Durkheimian Sociology: Cultural Studies*. Cambridge: Cambridge University Press.

Alexander, Jeffrey and Philip Smith (2001) The Strong Program in Cultural Theory: Elements of a Structural Hermeneutics. In J. Turner (Ed.), *Handbook of Social Theory*. New York: Kluwer Academic/Plenum Publishers, pp. 135–50.

Alexander, Jeffrey and Philip Smith (Eds) (2005) *The Cambridge Companion to Durkheim*. Cambridge: Cambridge University Press.

All Out (2012) 'Play Like a Girl' – The New Olympic Rule. Retrieved on 23 January 2013 from: http://www.allout.org/olympics

Ameel, Lieven and Sirpa Tani (2012) Everyday Aesthetics in Action: Parkour Eyes and the Beauty of Concrete Walls. *Emotion, Space and Society*, 5: 164–73.

Anderson, Robert and Wesley Sharrock (1993) Can Organisations Afford Knowledge? *Computer-Supported Cooperative Work*, 1: 143–61.

Ansdell, Gary and Mercédes Pavlicevic (2010) Practising 'Gentle Empiricism': The Nordoff-Robbins Research Heritage. *Music Therapy Perspectives*, 28 (2): 131–9.

Ansdell, Gary, Jane Davidson, Wendy L. Magee, John Meehan and Simon Procter (2010) From 'This F★★★ing Life' to 'That's Better'… in Four Minutes: An Interdisciplinary Study of Music Therapy's 'Present Moments' and Their Potential for Affect Modulation. *Nordic Journal of Music Therapy*, 19 (1): 3–28.

Appadurai, Arjun (Ed.) (1986) *The Social Life of Things: Commodities in Cultural Perspective.* Cambridge: Cambridge University Press.

Appelbaum, David (1995) *The Stop.* Albany, NY: SUNY Press.

Atkinson, Paul (1988) Ethnomethodology: A Critical Review. *Annual Review of Sociology*, 14: 441–65.

Atkinson, Paul (2006) *Everyday Arias.* Walnut Creek, CA: Alta Mira.

Atkinson, Paul (2013) Blowing Hot: The Ethnography of Craft and the Craft of Ethnography. *Qualitative Inquiry*, 19 (5): 397–404.

Atkinson, Paul, Amanda Coffey, Sara Delamont, John Lofland and Lyn Lofland (2001) *Handbook of Ethnography.* London: Sage.

Barnes, Barry (1982) On the Extension of Concepts and the Growth of Knowledge. *Sociological Review*, 30 (1): 23–44.

Batt-Rawden, Kari Bjerke (2006) Music – A Strategy to Promote Health in Rehabilitation? An Evaluation of Participation in a 'Music and Health Promotion Project'. *International Journal of Rehabilitation Research*, 29 (2): 171–3.

Beard, Mary (2012) What I See in the Mirror. *The Guardian* (30 April). Retrieved on 3 May 2013 from: http://www.guardian.co.uk/fashion/2012/mar/30/mary-beard-what-see-in-mirror

Beard, Mary (2013) Is My Name a Real Laugh? Question Time Feedback. *A Don's Life* (19 January). Retrieved on 31 January 2013 from: http://timesonline.typepad.com/dons_life/2013/01/is-my-name-a-real-laugh-question-time-feedback.html

Becker, Howard S. (1953) Becoming a Marihuana User. *American Journal of Sociology*, 59 (3): 235-242.

Bellah, Robert, Richard Madsen, William M. Sullivan, Ann Swidler and Steven M. Tipton (1985) *Habits of the Heart: Individualism and Commitment in American Life.* Berkeley, Los Angeles and London: University of California Press.

Berger, Bennett (2003 [1981]) *Survival of a Counterculture: Ideological Work and Everyday Life Among Rural Communards.* Livingston, NJ: Transaction Publishers.

Bijker, Wiebe E., Thomas P. Hughes and Trevor J. Pinch (Eds) (1989) *The Social Construction of Technological Systems: New Directions in the Sociology and History of Technology.* Cambridge, MA: MIT Press.

Birke, Lynda (1992a) Transforming Biology. In H. Crowley and S. Himmelweit (Eds), *Knowing Women: Feminism and Knowledge*. Cambridge: Polity, pp. 66–77.

Birke, Lynda (1992b) In Pursuit of Difference: Scientific Studies of Me and Women. In G. Kirkup and L. Smith Keller (Eds), *Inventing Women: Science, Technology and Gender*. Cambridge: Polity, pp. 81–102.

Bourdieu, Pierre (1977) *Outline of a Theory of Practice*. Cambridge: Cambridge University Press.

Bourdieu, Pierre (1984) *Distinction: A Social Critique of the Judgement of Taste*. Cambridge, MA: Harvard University Press.

Butler, Judith (2006 [1990]) *Gender Trouble: Feminism and the Subversion of Identity*. London: Routledge.

Cage, John (2009) *Listen*. Documentary film by Miroslav Sebestik. Transcript retrieved on 3 February 2013 from: http://hearingvoices.com/news/2009/09/cage-silence/

Camic, Paul (2010) From Trashed to Treasured: A Grounded Theory of the Found Object. *Psychology of Aesthetics, Creativity and the Arts*, 24 (2): 81–92.

Charmaz, Kathy (1991) *Good Days, Bad Days: Illness and Time*. New Brunswick, NJ: Rutgers University Press.

Christie, Agatha (1993 [1952]) *They Do It With Mirrors*. London: HarperCollins.

Christie, Agatha (2001 [1941]) *Evil Under The Sun*. London: HarperCollins.

Cicourel, Aaron V. (1964) *Method and Measurement in Sociology*. New York: The Free Press of Glencoe.

Cicourel, Aaron V. (1974) *Cognitive Sociology: Language and Meaning in Social Interaction*. New York: The Free Press.

Cicourel, Aaron V. (1996) Ecological Validity and 'White Room Effects': The Interaction of Cognitive and Cultural Models in the Pragmatic Analysis of Elicited Narratives from Children. *Pragmatics and Cognition*, 4 (2): 221–64.

Clark, Andy and David J. Chalmers (1998) The Extended Mind. *Analysis*, 58 (1): 10–23.

Collins, Randal (2004) *Interaction Ritual Chains*. Princeton, NJ: Princeton University Press.

Conrad, Peter (1987) The Experience of Illness. *Research in the Sociology of Health Care*, 1/6: 1–31.

Conrad, Peter (2007) *The Medicalization of Society: On the Transformation of Human Conditions into Treatable Disorders*. Baltimore: Johns Hopkins University Press.

Crossley, Nick (2001) *The Social Body: Habit, Identity and Desire*. London: Sage.

Csikszentmihalyi, Mihaly (1990) *Flow: The Psychology of Optimal Experience*. London: HarperCollins.

Csikszentmihalyi, Mihaly and Isabella Selega Csikszentmihalyi (Eds) (1988) *Optimal Experience: Psychological Studies of Flow in Consciousness*. Cambridge: Cambridge University Press.

de Certeau, Michel (2011 [1984]) *The Practice of Everyday Life* (3rd revised edn). Berkeley, Los Angeles and London: University of California Press.

de la Fuente, Eduardo (2007) The 'New Sociology of Art': Putting Art Back into Social Science Approaches to the Arts. *Cultural Sociology*, 1 (3): 409–25.

Delamont, Sara (1989) *Knowledgeable Women: Structuralism and the Reproduction of Elites*. London: Routledge.

Delamont, Sara (2006) The Smell of Sweat and Rum: Teacher Authority in Capoeira Classes. *Ethnography and Education*, 1 (2): 161–75.

Delamont, Sara and Neil Stephens (2008) Up on the Roof: The Embodied Habitus of Diasporic Capoiera. *Cultural Sociology*, 2 (1): 57–74.

DeNora, Tia (1986) How is Extra Musical Meaning Possible? Music as a Place and Space for 'Work'. *Sociological Theory*, 4 (1): 84–94.

DeNora, Tia (1995) *Beethoven and the Construction of Genius: Musical Politics in Vienna, 1792–1803*. Berkeley, Los Angeles and London: University of California Press.

DeNora, Tia (1996) From Physiology to Feminism: Reconfiguring Body, Gender and Expertise in Natural Fertility Control. *International Sociology*, 11 (3): 359–83.

DeNora, Tia (2000) *Music in Everyday Life*. Cambridge: Cambridge University Press.

DeNora, Tia (2003) *After Adorno: Rethinking Music Sociology*. Cambridge: Cambridge University Press.

DeNora, Tia (2006) Evidence and Effectiveness in Music Therapy. *British Journal of Music Therapy*, 20 (2): 81–99.

DeNora, Tia (2011 [1997]) Music and Erotic Agency: Sonic Resources and Social-Sexual Action. *Music-in-Action: Selected Essays in Sonic Ecology*. Farnham: Ashgate.

DeNora, Tia (2012) Resounding the Great Divide: Music in Everyday Life at the End of Life. *Mortality*, 17 (2): 92–105.

DeNora, Tia (2013) *Music Asylums: Wellbeing Through Music in Everyday Life*. Farnham: Ashgate.

Dewey, John (1934) *Art as Experience*. New York: Berkeley.

Dissanayake, Ellen (1988) *What Is Art For?* Seattle: University of Washington Press.

Douglas, Jack D. (Ed.) (1971) *Understanding Everyday Life: Toward the Reconstruction of Sociological Knowledge*. London: Routledge and Kegan Paul.

Douglas, Mary (2002 [1966]) *Purity and Danger: An Analysis of the Concepts of Pollution and Taboo*. London: Routledge.

Duchowski, Andrew T. (2007) *Eye Tracking Methodology: Theory and Practice* (2nd edn). London: Springer.

Durkheim, Emile (1982 [1895]) *The Rules of Sociological Method*. New York: The Free Press.

Durkheim, Emile (2001 [1912]) *The Elementary Forms of Religious Life*, Carol Cosman (Trans.). Oxford: Oxford University Press.

Fausto-Sterling, Anne (1993) The Five Sexes: Why Male and Female Are Not Enough. *The Sciences*, March/April: 20–4.

Feld, Steven (2012) *Sound and Sentiment: Birds, Weeping, Poetics, and Song in Kaluli Expression* (3rd edn). Philadelphia: University of Pennsylvania Press.

Fine, Gary Alan (1995) Wittgenstein's Kitchen: Sharing Meaning in Restaurant Work. *Theory and Society*, 24 (2): 245–69.

Fine, Gary Alan (2010) The Sociology of the Local: Action and its Publics. *Sociological Theory*, 28 (4): 356–76.

Fiske, Susan T. and Shelley E. Taylor (1984) *Social Cognition* (1st edn). Reading, MA: Addison-Wesley.

Fox Keller, Evelyn (1983) *A Feeling for the Organism: The Life and Work of Barbara McClintock*. New York: Henry Holt and Company.

Frake, Charles, O. (1997) Plying Frames Can Be Dangerous. In M. Cole, Y. Engeström and O. Vasquez (Eds), *Mind, Culture and Activity: Seminal Papers From the Laboratory of Comparative Human Cognition*. Cambridge: Cambridge University Press, pp. 32–49.

Freund, Peter (2001) Bodies, Disabilities and Spaces: The Social Model and Disabling Spatial Organisations. *Disability and Society*, 16 (5): 689–706.

Frith, Simon (1990) Afterthoughts. In S. Frith and A. Goodwin (Eds), *On Record: Rock, Pop and the Written Word*. London: Routledge, pp. 359–65.

Fryer, Jane (2013) How I Turned the Tables on my Trolls: Mary Beard Suffered Vile Online Abuse about her Looks after Appearing on Question Time. *Mail Online* (26 January). Retrieved on 3 May 2013 from: http://www.dailymail.co.uk/news/article-2268558/How-I-turned-tables-trolls-Mary-Beard-suffered-vile-online-abuse-looks-appearing-Question-Time.html

Gabriel, Norman and Stephen Mennell (Eds) (2011) *Norbert Elias and Figurational Research: Processual Thinking in Sociology*. Oxford: Wiley Blackwell.

Gagnon, John and William Simon (1974) *Sexual Conduct: The Social Sources of Human Sexuality*. London: Hutchinson & Co.

Garfinkel, Harold (1967) *Studies in Ethnomethodology*. New York: The Free Press.

Garfinkel, Harold (2002) *Ethnomethodology's Program: Working Out Durkheim's Aphorism*. Lanham, MD: Rowman and Littlefield.

Garfinkel, Harold, Michael Lynch and Eric Livingston (1981) The Work of a Discovering Science Construed with Materials from the Optically Discovered Pulsar. *Philosophy of the Social Sciences*, 11: 131–58.

Geertz, Clifford (1973) *Thick Description: Toward an Interpretive Theory of Culture: The Interpretation of Cultures*. New York: Basic Books.

Gell, Alfred (1992) Technology of Enchantment and Enchantment of Technology. In J. Coote and A. Shelton (Eds), *Art and Aesthetics*. Oxford: Oxford University Press, pp. 40–67.

Goffman, Erving (1959) *The Presentation of Self in Everyday Life*. New York: Doubleday.

Goffman, Erving (1961) *Asylums: Essays on the Social Situation of Mental Patients and Other Inmates*. New York: Anchor.

Goffman, Erving (1986 [1977]) *Frame Analysis: An Essay on the Organization of Experience*. Boston: Northeastern University Press.

Gomart, Emilie and Antone Hennion (1999) A Sociology of Attachment: Music Amateurs, Drug Users. In J. Hassard and J. Law (Eds), *ANT and After* (Sociological Review Monograph). Oxford: Blackwell, pp. 220–47.

Gouk, Penelope (2000) *Musical Healing in Cultural Context*. Farnham: Ashgate.

Groce, Nora (2006 [1988]) *Everyone Here Spoke Sign Language: Hereditary Deafness on Martha's Vineyard*. Cambridge, MA: Harvard University Press.

Gusfield, Joseph (2000) *Performing Action: Artistry in Human Behavior and Social Research*. Piscataway, NJ: Transaction Publishers.

Hacking, Ian (1995) *Rewriting the Soul: Multiple Personality and the Sciences of Memory*. Princeton, NJ: Princeton University Press.

Hacking, Ian (1999) *The Social Construction of What?* Cambridge, MA: Harvard University Press.

Hanser, Suzanne B. (2010) Music, Health, and Well-Being. In P. Juslin and J. Sloboda (Eds), *Handbook of Music and Emotion*. Oxford: Oxford University Press, pp. 849–77.

Hara, Mariko (2011) Expanding a Care Network for People with Dementia and Their Carers Through Musicking: Participant Observation with 'Singing for the Brain'. *Voices: A World Forum for Music Therapy*, 11 (2). Retrieved on 29 February 2013 from: https://normt.uib.no/index.php/voices/rt/printerFriendly/570/459

Hara, Mariko and Tia DeNora (2013) Leaving Something to the Imagination: 'Seeing' New Places through a Musical Lens. In J. Richardson and C. Vernallis (Eds), *Oxford Handbook of New Audiovisual Aesthetics*. Oxford: Oxford University Press, pp. 659–72.

Harrington, Brooke and Gary Alan Fine (2006) Where the Action is: Small Groups and Recent Developments in Sociological Theory. *Small Group Research*, 37 (1): 4–19.

Heider, Karl G. (1988) The Rashomon Effect: When Ethnographers Disagree. *American Anthropologist*, 90(1) (March): 73-81.

Hennion, Antoine (2004) Pragmatics of Taste. In M. Jacobs and N. Hanrahan (Eds), *The Blackwell Companion to the Sociology of Culture*. Cambridge, MA: Blackwell, pp. 131–44.

Hennion, Antoine (2007) Those Things that Hold Us Together. *Cultural Sociology*, 1 (1): 97–114.

Heritage, John (1984) *Garfinkel and Ethnomethodology*. Cambridge: Polity Press.

Hetherington, Kevin (2002) The Unsightly: Visual Impairment, Touch and the Parthenon Frieze. *Theory, Culture and Society*, 19 (5–6): 187–205.

Hetherington, Kevin (2003) Accountability and Disposal: Visual Impairment and the Museum. *Museum and Society*, 1 (2): 104–15.

Hilbert, Richard (1986) Anomie and the Moral Regulation of Reality: The Durkheimian Tradition in Modern Relief. *Sociological Theory*, 4 (1): 1–19.

Hochschild, Arlie R. (1979) Emotion Work, Feeling Rules, and Social Structure. *American Journal of Sociology*, 85 (3): 551–75.

Holland, Dorothy, William Lachicotte Jr, Debra Skinner and Carole Cain (1998) *Identity and Agency in Cultural Worlds*. Cambridge, MA: Harvard University Press.

Holmqvist, Kenneth, Marcus Nyström, Richard Andersson, Richard Dewhurst, Halszka Jarodzka and Joost van de Weijer (2011) *Eye Tracking: A Comprehensive Guide to Methods and Measures*. Oxford: Oxford University Press.

Horden, Peregrine (2000) *Music as Medicine*. Farnham: Ashgate.

Hudson, J.L. (2013) J.L. Hudson, Seedsman (A Public Access Seed Bank). Catalogue. Retrieved on 13 May 2013 from: http://www.jlhudsonseeds.net/VegetablesS-Z.htm

Hurley, Patrick J. (2008) *A Concise Introduction to Logic* (10th edn). Belmont, CA: Thompson.

Hutchins, Edwin (1995) *Cognition in the Wild*. Cambridge, MA: MIT Press.

Inglis, David (2005) *Culture and Everyday Life*. London: Routledge.

Inglis, David (2013) What is Worth Defending in Sociology Today? Presentism, Historical Vision and the Uses of Sociology. *Cultural Sociology*, 7 (1): 1–20.

Ingold, Tim (2000) *Perception of the Environment: Essays in Livelihood, Dwelling, and Skill*. London: Routledge.

Jackson, Stevi and Sue Scott (2007) Faking Like a Woman? Towards an Interpretive Theorization of Sexual Pleasure. *Body and Society*, 13 (2): 95–116.

Jacobs, Mark (1990) *Screwing the System and Making it Work: Juvenile Justice in the No-Fault Society*. Chicago: University of Chicago Press.

James, William (1950) The Perception of Reality. *Principles of Psychology*, Vol. 2. New York: Dover Publications, pp. 283–324.

James, William (1981) *Principles of Psychology*. Cambridge, MA: Harvard University Press.

Juniper, Andrew (2003) *Wabi Sabi: The Japanese Art of Impermanence*. Boston: Tuttle Publishing.

Katsanos, Christos, Nikolaos Tsellos and Nikolaos Avouris (2010) Evaluating Website Navigability: Validation of a Tool-based Approach through Two Eye-tracking User Studies. *New Review of Hypermedia and Multimedia*, 16 (1–2): 195–214.

Katzen, Molly (2000) *The New Moosewood Cookbook*. New York: Ten Speed Press.

Kovic, Vanja, Kim Plunkett and Gert Westernmann (2009) Eye-Tracking Study of Inanimate Objects. *Psihologija*, 42 (4): 417–36.

Langer, Ellen J. (2009) *Counterclockwise: Mindful Health and the Power of Possibility*. New York: Random House.

Laqueur, Thomas (1990) *Making Sex: Body and Gender from the Greeks to Freud*. Cambridge, MA: Harvard University Press.

Latour, Bruno (1987) *Science in Action: How to Follow Scientists and Engineers Through Society*. Cambridge, MA: Harvard University Press.

Latour, Bruno (1988) A Relativistic Account of Einstein's Relativity. *Social Studies of Science*, 18 (1): 3–44.

Latour, Bruno (2005) *Reassembling the Social: An Introduction to Actor-Network-Theory*. Oxford: Oxford University Press.

Latour, Bruno (2011) What's the Story? Organizing as a Mode of Existence. In J.-H. Passoth, B. Peuker and M. Schillmeier (Eds), *Agency Without Actors? New Approaches to Collective Action*. London: Routledge, pp. 163–78.

Latour, Bruno and Steve Woolgar (1986 [1979]) *Laboratory Life: The Construction of Scientific Facts*. Princeton, NJ: Princeton University Press.

Law, John (2002) *Aircraft Stories: Decentering the Object in Technoscience*. Durham, NC: Duke University Press.

Law, John (2004) *After Method: Mess in Social Science Research*. London: Routledge.

Law, John and Annemarie Mol (2001) Situating Technoscience: An Inquiry into Spatialities. *Society and Space*, 19 (5): 609–21.

Lefebvre, Henri (1971 [1968]) *Everyday Life in the Modern World*, S. Rabinovitch (Trans.). London: Allen Lane.

Legrand, Dorothee (2007) Pre-reflective Self-consciousness: On Being Bodily in the World. *Consciousness and Cognition*, 16 (3): 687–99.

Lemert, Charles (2002) The Pleasure of Garfinkel's Indexical Ways. In H. Garfinkel, *Ethnomethodology's Program: Working out Durkheim's Aphorism*. Lanham, MD: Rowman and Littlefield, pp. i–x.

Liddle, Rod (2013) It's not Misogyny, Professor Beard: It's You. *The Spectator* (26 January). Retrieved on 31 January 2013 from: http://www.spectator.co.uk/columnists/rod-liddle/8830261/its-not-misogyny-professor-beard-its-you/

Linstead, Stephen (2006) Ethnomethodology and Sociology: An Introduction. *The Sociological Review*, 54 (3): 399–404.

Luker, Kristin (1984) *Abortion and the Politics of Motherhood*. Berkeley, Los Angeles and London: University of California Press.

Mack, Adrien and Irvin Rock (1998) *Inattentional Blindness*. Cambridge, MA: MIT Press.

MacKenzie, Donald A. and Judy Wajcman (1999 [1985]) *The Social Shaping of Technology*. London: Open University Press.

Macknik, Stephen and Susanna Martinex-Conde (2011) *Sleights of Mind: What the Neuroscience of Magic Reveals About Our Brains*. London: Profile Books.

Malcolm X (2007 [1965]) *The Autobiography of Malcolm X*. New York: Penguin.

Marland, Hilary (1999) At Home with Puerperal Mania: The Domestic Treatment of the Insanity of Childbirth in the Nineteenth Century, in Peter Bartlett and David Wright (Eds), *Outside the Walls of the Asylum: The History of Care in the Community 1750–2000*. London and New Brunswick, NJ: Athlone, pp. 45–65.

Marland, Hilary (2004) *Dangerous Motherhood: Insanity and Childbirth in Victorian Britain*. Basingstoke: Palgrave Macmillan.

Marvel, Andrew (n.d. [c.1650]) To his Coy Mistress. The Poetry Foundation. Retrieved on 30 April 2013 from: http://www.poetryfoundation.org/poem/173954

Marx, Karl (1972 [1852]) The Eighteenth Brumaire of Napolean Bonaparte. *The Karl Marx Library*, Vol. 1, Saul K. Padover (Ed.). New York: McGraw-Hill.

Marx, Karl (1998 [1845]) *The German Ideology* [including the theses on Feurbach]. New York: Prometheus Books.

Marx, Karl (2008 [1847]) *The Poverty of Philosophy: Answer to the Philosophy of Poverty by M. Proudhon*. New York: Cosimo Books.

Mauss, Marcel (1992) Techniques of the Body. In Jonathan Crary and Sanford Kwinter (Eds), *Incorporations*. New York: Zone, pp. 455–77.

Maynard, Douglas and Steven E. Clayman (1991) The Diversity of Ethnomethodology. *Annual Review of Sociology*, 17: 385–418.

Mazzotti, Massimo (2004) Enlightened Mills: Mechanizing Olive Oil Production in Mediterranean Europe. *Technology and Culture*, 45 (2): 277–304.

McCormick, Lisa (2009) Higher, Faster, Louder: Representations of the International Music Competition. *Cultural Sociology*, 3 (5): 5–30.

Mehan, Hugh (1990) Oracular Reasoning in a Psychiatric Exam: The Resolution of Conflict in Language. In A. Grimshaw (Ed.), *Conflict Talk: Sociolinguistic Investigations of Arguments in Conversations*. Cambridge: Cambridge University Press, pp. 160–77.

Miller, Daniel (2010) *Stuff*. Cambridge: Polity Press.

Mills, C. Wright (2000 [1959]) *The Sociological Imagination*. Oxford: Oxford University Press.

Mol, Annemarie (2002) *The Body Multiple: Ontology in Medical Practice*. Durham, NC: Duke University Press.

Molotch, Harvey (2005) *Where Stuff Comes From: How Toasters, Toilets, Cars, Computers and Many Other Things Come To Be As They Are*. London: Routledge.

Montgomery, Hugh (2011) Bocca Cookbook. Cook the books: 'Independent on Sunday' Writers Recreate Dishes from the Year's Most Fashionable Cookbooks. *The Independent on Sunday* (4 December). Retrieved on 22

January 2013 from: http://www.independent.co.uk/life-style/food-and-drink/features/cook-the-books-independent-on-sunday-writers-recreate-dishes-from-the-years-most-fashionable-cookbooks-6270567.html

Moran, Joe (2005) *Reading the Everyday*. London: Routledge.

Mukerji, Chandra (2009) *Impossible Engineering: Technology and Territoriality on the Canal du Midi*. Princeton, NJ: Princeton University Press.

Myung-Ok Lee, Marie (2011) Designer Vagina Surgery: Snip, Stitch, Kerching! *The Guardian* (14 October).

Norman, Donald (2002 [1988]) *The Design of Everyday Things*. New York: Basic Books. (Original title: *The Psychology of Everyday Things*.)

Pavlicevic, Mercédès and Gary Ansdell (Eds) (2004) *Community Music Therapy*. London: Jessica Kingsley.

Pickering, Andrew (1995) *The Mangle of Practice*. Chicago: University of Chicago Press.

Pickering, Andrew (2010) *The Cybernetic Brain: Sketches of Another Future*. Chicago: University of Chicago Press.

Pink, Sarah (2004) *Home Truths: Gender, Domestic Objects and Everyday Life*. Oxford: Berg.

Pink, Sarah (2012) *Situating Everyday Life*. London: Sage.

Pleasants, Nigel (1999) *Wittgenstein and the Idea of a Critical Social Theory: A Critique of Giddens, Habermas and Bhaskar*. London: Routledge.

Pollner, Melvin (1987) *Mundane Reason: Reality in Everyday and Sociological Discourse*. Cambridge: Cambridge University Press.

Porter, Roy (1997) *The Greatest Benefit to Mankind: A Medical History of Humanity*. London: Harper Collins.

Procter, Simon (2011) Reparative Musicing: Thinking on the Usefulness of Social Capital Theory within Music Therapy. *Nordic Journal of Music Therapy*, 20 (3): 242–62.

Reed, Isaac (2007) Why Salem Made Sense: Culture, Gender, and the Puritan Persecution of Witchcraft. *Cultural Sociology*, 1 (2): 209–34.

Reed, Issac (2011) *Interpretation and Social Knowledge: On the Use of Theory in the Social Sciences*. Chicago: University of Chicago Press.

Reid Smith, Tris (2012) Activists Protest Olympic 'Gender Police' over Sex Tests. *GayStarNews* (26 July). Retrieved on 23 January 2013 from: http://www.gaystarnews.com/article/activists-protest-olympic-'gender-police'-over-sex-tests260712

Rojek, Chris (2011) *Pop Music, Pop Culture*. Cambridge: Polity.

Rosenhan, David (1973) On Being Sane in Insane Places. *Science*, 179: 250–8.

Ruud, Even (2005) Music: A Salutogenic Way to Health Promotion? In G. Tellnes (Ed.), *Urbanisation and Health: New Challenges in Health Promotion and Prevention*. Oslo: Unipubforlag, pp. 143–50.

Saferstein, Barry (2007) Process Narratives, Grey Boxes, and Discourse Frameworks: Cognition, Interaction, and Constraint in Understanding Genetics and Medicine. *European Journal of Social Theory*, 10 (3): 424–47.

Saferstein, Barry (2010) Cognitive Sociology. In J. Jaspers, J.-O. Östman and J. Verschueren (Eds), *Society and Language Use*. Amsterdam: John Benjamins, pp. 113–26.

Schillmeier, Michael (2008) Time-Spaces of In/dependence and Dis/ability. *Time and Society*, 17 (2/3): 215–31.

Schillmeier, Michael (2010) *Rethinking Dis/ability*. London: Routledge.

Schutz, Alfred (1945) On Multiple Realities. *Philosophy and Phenomenological Research*, 5 (4): 533–76.

Schutz, Alfred (1951) Making Music Together – A Study in Social Relationship. *Social Research: An International Quarterly*, 18 (1): 76–97.

Scott, Susie (2006) The Medicalization of Shyness: From Social Misfits to Social Fitness. *Sociology of Health and Illness*, 28 (2): 133–53.

Scott, Susie (2009) *Making Sense of Everyday Life*. Cambridge: Polity.

Scott, Sue and Jackson, Stevi (2010) *Theorising Sexuality*. Maiden Hill: Open University Press.

Sennett, Richard (2008) *The Craftsman*. London: Penguin Books.

Sennett, Richard (2012) *Together: The Rituals, Pleasures and Politics of Co-operation*. New Haven, CT: Yale University Press.

Shea, Christopher (2012) British TV Critic Deems Cambridge Classicist Insufficiently Attractive. *The Wall Street Journal* (20 April). Retrieved on 31 January 2013 from: http://blogs.wsj.com/ideas-market/2012/04/23/british-tv-critic-deems-cambridge-classicist-insufficiently-attractive/

Shakespeare, William (1992) *Hamlet*. Wordsworth Edition.

Shotter, John (1993) *Cultural Politics of Everyday Life: Social Constructionism, Rhetoric and Knowing of the Third Kind*. Toronto: University of Toronto Press.

Simons, Daniel J. and Christopher F. Chabris (1999) Gorillas in our Midst: Sustained Inattentional Blindness for Dynamic Events. *Perception*, 28 (9): 1059–74.

Smart, Carol (2007) *Personal Life*. Cambridge: Polity.

Star, Susan Leigh and James R. Griesemer (1989) Institutional Ecology, 'Translations' and Boundary Objects: Amateurs and Professionals in Berkeley's Museum of Vertebrate Zoology, 1907–39. *Social Studies of Science*, 19 (3): 387–420.

Stige, Brynjulf, Gary Ansdell, Cochavit Elefant and Mercédès Pavlicevic (2010) *Where Music Helps: Community Music Therapy in Action and Reflection*. Farnham: Ashgate.

Stoller, Paul (1997) *Sensuous Scholarship*. Philadelphia: University of Pennsylvania Press.

Strati, Antonio (1999) *Organization and Aesthetics*. London: Sage.

Strati, Antonio (2008) Aesthetics in the Study of Organizational Life. In D. Barry and H. Hansen (Eds), *The Sage Handbook of New Approaches in Management and Organization*. London: Sage, pp. 229–38.

Streeck, Jurgan (1996) How to Do Things with Things. *Human Studies*, 19: 365–84.

Suchman, Lucy (2005) Affiliative Objects. *Organization*, 12 (3): 379–99.

Sutherland, Ian and Sophia Acord (2007) Thinking with Art: From Situated Knowledge to Experiential Knowing. *Journal of Visual Art Practice*, 6 (2): 125–40.

Szasz, Thomas (1960) The Myth of Mental Illness. *American Psychologist*, 15: 113–18.

The Metro (2012) Pixie Lott and Julia Roberts: Celebrity Armpit Hair Face Off. (20 July). Retrieved on 1 February 2013 from: http://metro.co.uk/2012/07/20/pixie-lott-and-julia-roberts-celebrity-armpit-hair-face-off-503401/

Thomas, William I. and Dorothy S. Thomas (1928) *The Child in America: Behavior Problems and Programs.* New York: Knopf.

Thoreau, Henry David (1986 [1854]) *Walden and Civil Disobedience.* New York: Penguin.

Thrift, Nigel (2008) *Non-representational Theory: Space|Politics|Affect.* London: Routledge.

Tota, Anna Lisa (2004) Museums and the Public Representation of Other Cultures: The Ethnic Exhibitions. *Studies in Communication Sciences*, 4 (1): 201–18.

Tota, Anna Lisa (2005) Counter-memories of Terrorism: The Public Inscription of a Dramatic Past. In Mark D. Jacobs and Nancy Weiss Hanrahan (Eds), *The Blackwell Companion to the Sociology of Culture.* Oxford: Blackwell, pp. 272–85.

Trevarthen, Colwyn (1977) Descriptive Analyses of Infant Communicative Behavior. In H.R. Schafer (Ed.), *Studies in Mother–Infant Interaction.* London: Academic Press, pp. 227–70.

Trevarthen, Colwyn (2010) What is it Like to Be a Person Who Knows Nothing? Defining the Active Intersubjective Mind of a Newborn Human Being. *Infant and Child Development*, 29 (1): 119–35. Retrieved on 2 May 2013 from: http://www.psych.uw.edu.pl/lasc/Trevarthen2.pdf

Tudhope, D.S. and J.V. Oldfield (1982) A High-Level Recognizer for Schematic Diagrams. *Computer Graphics and Applications*, 3 (3): 33–40.

Turner, Bryan S. (1995) *Medical Power and Social Knowledge* (2nd edn). London: Sage.

Turner, Bryan S. (2008) Religious Speech: The Ineffable Nature of Religious Communication in the Information Age. *Theory, Culture and Society*, 25 (7–8): 219–35.

Undateables, The Channel 4. Retrieved on 1 February 2013 from: http://www.channel4.com/programmes/the-undateables

Vannini, Phillip, Guppy Ahluwalia-Lopez, Dennis Waskul and Simon Gottschalk (2010) Performing Taste at Wine Festivals: A Somatic Layered Account of Material Culture. *Qualitative Inquiry*, 16 (5): 378–96.

Wacquant, Loïc (2004) *Body and Soul.* New York: Oxford University Press.

Wainwright, Steven P., Clare Williams and Bryan S. Turner (2006) Varieties of Habitus and the Embodiment of Ballet. *Qualitative Research*, 6 (4): 381–97.

Walton, Thomas (1996) The Argument of the Beard. *Informal Logic*, 18 (2–3): 235–59.

Warhurst, Chris, Dennis Nickson, Anne Witz and Anne Marie Cullen (2000) Aesthetic Labour in Interactive Service Work: Some Case Study Evidence from the 'New' Glasgow. *Service Industries Journal*, 20 (3): 1–18.

Warhurst, Chris, Diane van den Broek, Richard Hall and Dennis Nickson (2012) Great Expectations: Gender, Looks and Lookism at Work. *International Journal of Work Organisation and Emotion*, 5 (1): 72–90.

Warner, Marina (2012) What I See in the Mirror. *The Guardian* (2 November). Retrieved on 3 May 2013 from: http://www.guardian.co.uk/fashion/2012/nov/02/marina-warner-critic-writer-interview

Weber, Max (1978) *Economy and Society*, Guenther Roth and Claus Wittich (Trans.). Berkeley and Los Angeles: University of California Press.

Wieder, D. Lawrence (1971) On Meaning by Rule. In Jack D. Douglas (Ed.), *Understanding Everyday Life: Toward the Reconstruction of Sociological Knowledge*. London: Routledge and Kegan Paul, pp. 107–35.

Wieder, D. Lawrence (1974) *Language and Social Reality: The Case of Telling the Convict Code*. The Hague: Mouton. (Reprinted, University Press of America, 1988.)

Williams, Raymond (1976) *Keywords: A Vocabulary of Culture and Society*. London: Fontana Press.

Wilson-Kovacs, Dana (2007) Consumption and Sexual Intimacy: Towards an Understanding of Intimate Cultures in Everyday Life. In E. Casey and L. Martens (Eds), *Gender and Consumption: Domestic Cultures and the Commercialisation of Everyday Life*. Aldershot: Ashgate, pp. 181–95.

Wilson-Kovacs, Dana (2009) Some Texts Do it Better: Women, Sexually Explicit Texts and the Everyday. In F. Atwood (Ed.), *Mainstreaming Sex: The Sexualisation of Western Culture*. London: I.B. Tauris, pp. 147–65.

Wilson-Kovacs, Dana (2010) Class and Sexual Intimacy: An Everyday Life Perspective. In Y. Taylor (Ed.), *Classed Intersections: Spaces, Selves, Knowledges*. Farnham: Ashgate, pp. 217–35.

Winner, Langdon (1980) Do Artifacts Have Politics? *Dædalus*, 109 (1). (Reprinted in *The Social Shaping of Technology*, ed. Donald A. MacKenzie and Judy Wajcman, London: Open University Press, 1985; 2nd edn 1999.)

Wiseman, Frederick (1967) *Titicut Follies*. Zipporah Films, Inc.

Witkin, Robert W. (1994) *Art and Social Structure*. Cambridge: Polity.

Witkin, Robert (1998) *Adorno on Music*. London: Routledge.

Witkin, Robert (2000) Why did Adorno Hate Jazz? *Sociological Theory*, 18 (1): 134–70.

Witkin, Robert (2003) *Adorno on Popular Culture*. London: Routledge.

Witkin, Robert W. (2009) The Aesthetic Imperative of a Rational-Technical Machinery: A Study in Organizational Control Through the Design of Artifacts. *Music and Arts in Action*, 2 (1): 56–68.

Witkin, Robert and Tia DeNora (1997) Aesthetic Materials and Aesthetic Agency. *Newsletter of the Sociology of Culture Section of the American Sociological Association* 12 (1): 1–6.

Wittgenstein, Ludwig (1958) *Philosophische Untersuchungen/Philosophical Investigations*. Revised 4th edn. Oxford: Wiley-Blackwell.

Wittgenstein, Ludwig (1980) *Remarks on the Philosophy of Psychology*, Vol. I. Chicago: University of Chicago Press.

Wittgenstein, Ludwig (2001) *Tractatus Logico-Philosophicus*. London: Routledge.

Witz, Anne, Chris Warhurst and Dennis Nickson (2003) The Labour of Aesthetics and the Aesthetics of Organisation. *Organization*, 10 (1): 33–54.

Zimmerman, Don. H and D. Lawrence Wieder (1971) Ethnomethodology and the Problem of Order: Comment on Denzin. In Jack D. Douglas (Ed.), *Understanding Everyday Life: Toward the Reconstruction of Sociological Knowledge*. London: Routledge and Kegan Paul, pp. 285–98.

INDEX

terminal illness, variability of 61–2
They Do It With Mirrors (Christie)
    115–16, 118
Thomas Theorem 31, 33
time
    material practices in 146–9
    variations in space and 57–64
'too much reality', problem of
    44–7
Trevarthen, C. 132–3

Vannini, P. et al. 131–2
visual impairment 142–3

Wainwright, S.P. et al. 54
Walton, T. 24, 25
Warhurst, C. et al. 71
Weber, M. 67, 87
Wieder, D.L. 82
Wilson-Kovacs, D. 134–6, 137
Winner, L. 149
witch hunts
    Mary Beard 63–7
    Salem 42–4, 45, 57, 65
Witkin, R.W. 9–10, 71, 79
Wittgenstein, L. 5–8, 17, 19
    duck doodle 108, 109–10, 111–12

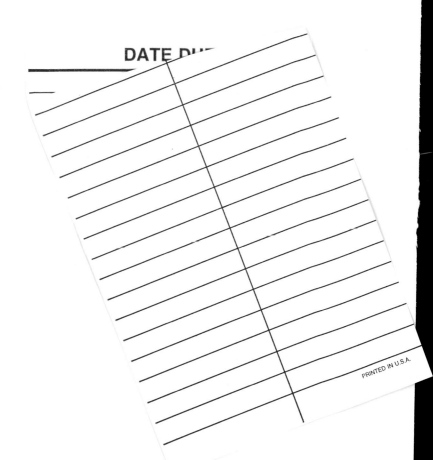

DATE DUE

PRINTED IN U.S.A.